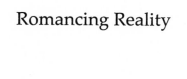

Romancing Reality

Romancing Reality

HomoViator and the Scandal Called Beauty

Marion Montgomery

ST. AUGUSTINE'S PRESS
South Bend, Indiana
2002

1 2 3 4 5 6 08 07 06 05 04 03 02

Library of Congress Cataloging in Publication Data
Montgomery, Marion.
    Romancing reality : homo viator and the scandal called
beauty / Marion Montgomery.
      p. cm.
    ISBN 1-58731-725-7 (alk. paper)
    1. Aesthetics. 2. Reality. I. Title.
BH39 .M592 2001
111'.85 – dc21   2001002575

∞ *The paper used in this publication meets the minimum requirements of the
International Organisation for Standardization (ISO) – Paper for
documents – Requirements for permanence – ISO 9706: 1994.*

Printed in the Czech Republic by Newton Printing Ltd.   www.newtonprinting .com

Contents

Preface

Tolstoy, in his "Conclusion" to *What Is Art?* champions art as "an organ of mankind's life" which "transmutes people's reasonable consciousness into feeling." Given the argument leading to that conclusion, one is surprised by his speaking of *"reasonable* consciousness," since reason is the great enemy to his desired end, namely a *"religious* consciousness of men" which is a "consciousness of brotherhood of man" against which reason proves subversive (emphasis added). What is necessary is a conversion of *reasonable* to *religious* consciousness, and that can only be accomplished by art's uses in making *feeling* dominant over reason. As for the agent to this transformation, the "true artist," he must be distinguished from the dominant pretenders, guilty of a Donatist heresy pervasive of the art world, where false artists are widely accepted as making true art. But one, with the eyes of the simple unlettered peasant before a work of art, can know at once the true from the false: the true artist and that beholding true person recognize as mutual between them, and as inescapable in the art in consequence, the overriding human virtue, "sincerity." It is through a stirring to mutuality, to a common "brotherhood," that true art is prescribed. In Tolstoy's terms, true art achieves an "infection" of man with common "feeling." What is required for the purification of that infecting instrument art is "sincerity." And so *feeling, sincerely* experienced by the artist and held as central to whatever art thing he makes, effects a work which must be declared good art, true art, and carrier of that "infection," true brotherhood.

Let us recall the argument out of Kant whose final persuasiveness comes to rest in a recognized sincerity in the philosopher. It grows out of Kant's concern in recognizing a problem attendant upon the philosopher's deportment in his intellectual actions. For as philosopher, he cannot be simply speculative in his detachment, engaging ideas or concepts in the subjunctive mode. He must exercise a "pure" neutrality (to borrow a favored Kantian adjective) toward the object of his reason, which turns out to be an object called *idea*. Thus his argument may attain a certain purity of reason, untainted by desire or intention. Indeed, such an intellectual deportment as philosopher is a necessity even at a practical level, for in philosophizing he communicates with minds whose reason is insufficiently purified, so that a persuasiveness is necessary, given the world of nature and human nature which Kant opposes in a reaction as philosopher. How does one justify "pure reason" to those held by that world? For that reason, if for no other, his is an argument to be made independent of the philosopher's personal interest or motivation, lest by that precedence of attitude the truth sought be a tainted truth. Argument must be unencumbered by personal cause, a condition to philosophical argument which Tolstoy applies as well to art's cause, since the personal is antipathetic to the universalism of brotherhood. Feeling must be a universal made pure by separating it from the particularities constituting specific persons.

And so that brings us again to a virtue common to Kant and Tolstoy. How is either philosopher or artist to make evident an impersonal devotion whose means is either pure reason or pure feeling? Jacques Maritain engages the concern, not in relation to the artist but directly in response to Kant's defense of reason as purified of the personal. (See Maritain's *Introduction to the Basic Problems of Moral Philosophy*.) How are we – mundane thinkers and not yet risen to the purity of thought whereby (as Kant will hold) a consistent illusion becomes the highest ground attainable to reason – how are we to achieve by impersonal devotion that consistency? From our side, listening to the philosopher, how may we recognize the disinterestedness of intellect which Kant requires of the philosopher?

We shall suggest in a long consideration of Tolstoy's ambiguous defense of art that, despite his studied attempt to do so, he never succeeds in exorcising from his mind the presence of Kant, whom he studied with enthusiasm early in life. And to this point, let us suggest a moral dimension of Kantian philosophy which in the end Tolstoy adapts to his moral dimension of art. For Kant, *disinterestedness* is the moral imperative to the philosopher, which one might discover evidenced – more or less – by the philosopher's *sincere* indifference to the consequences of his argument as that argument might affect him "personally." Indeed, the consequences of philosophical consistency, adumbrated by Kant as possible only in the region of illusion (the region of a universalism projected by reason as the necessity to consistency) may very well leave the person much troubled personally by reason's dictation of his devotion to intellectual illusion, difficult to reconcile to the present-seeming reality of person in the world.

In the face of this dilemma, Kant holds to the moral high ground as philosopher, holds to the virtue of disinterestedness. He does so with the expectation, Jacques Maritain suggests, that we his followers may be reassured insofar as we recognize in him the philosopher's sincerity, especially so in regard to his judgments within the arena of morality governing social affairs. There, freedom of choice sincerely made becomes (says Maritain) "the material element of morality," judged in respect to formal actions according to sincerity in the exercise of freedom by the will. Such is the murky climate descended upon human circumstances in the social world out of Kantian pursuits of a consistency of thought which at last he sees as possible only in that abstract region of universalism established by reason's angelism.

If Tolstoy brings the same climate of thought seemingly closer to home, relating it to the "brotherhood of man" – to be accomplished through "true science" as translated by "true art" into an "infectious" universal "feeling" dissolving persons into a brotherhood – Tolstoy's is no less an abstractionism posited through "pure feeling" than Kant's abstractionism in pursuit of "pure reason." And this is to suggest two points. The lesser is that Tolstoy himself has not escaped Kantian philosophy as he struggled to do. More importantly, it is to suggest one of the extremes to which Kantian thought devolves us, in our multitude of Kantian effects upon thought. To see one Western example of this effect, in comparison to the Eastern example in Tolstoy, we might look into German Romanticism. And for the purpose of relating the species of Kantian effects more ordinately, we shall consider Friedrich Schiller as poet turned philosopher, related by his argument to Tolstoy as a poet turned secular theologian. Schiller's *Letters on the Aesthetic Education of Man* thus proves an interesting preamble, anticipating Tolstoy's *What Is Art?* by a hundred years.

After considering Tolstoy as representative of the poet becoming secular theologian, though in his own mind he is consummate Christian, we shall turn to a more radical perspective in response – a root reaction evident in our arguments presenting a kinship of Schiller and Tolstoy. There the central concern will be art in its supportive role to the pilgrim person on his way. But to do so, we shall address that always vexing and fascinating problem to intellect, the problem of beauty. For, however variously *homo viator* responds to the effect of beauty upon him, it is a response to a haunting residue of effect in consciousness from his encounters with the world in which he travels, which world in their differing ways both Kant and Tolstoy would set aside. Beauty makes consciousness restless, and it finds itself torn between faring beyond this moment or settling into this moment in an arrest

as if thereby it might hold an ambiguous "something" desired
– a something stirring a longing through beauty for a something larger than beauty as limited to sensual experience of
this world.

Our radical – our root – engagement of this mystery to our
faring the world we shall attempt as it was engaged long ago
by Thomas Aquinas and more recently by Etienne Gilson and
Jacques Maritain as philosophers; and by certain of our poets
from Homer to G. M. Hopkins and T. S. Eliot. It is that mystery defined by Thomas as at last touching our very moral
nature: *id quod visum placet*; beauty is that which when seen
pleases. In our concern, we shall, then, address this mystery
primarily with this philosopher's help. Both Gilson and
Maritain, indeed, as philosophers reintroduce a concern for
the "science" of aesthetics as they take a firm position against
intellect's disorientation by post-Cartesian idealism from a
fundamental realism justified through what we often call
"common sense." For both, the idealism they oppose is a
species differing from Plato's. It is a new species of idealism
become dominant in Western philosophy since Descartes.
And indeed, it is in reaction to this new Western idealism that
Tolstoy himself rages, but in doing so he would cast all
Western science and Western philosophy into outer darkness.

Gilson recognizes the *cul de sac* into which modern
Western philosophy has lured intellect, and he reacts as does
Tolstoy but toward a radically differing solution. He does so
on firmer intellectual grounds than Tolstoy's, recognizing the
dangers of an incipient Manichaeanism in the new idealism
which Tolstoy does not escape. Gilson's is in reaction to the
distorted ends championed by Modernism as if proper to
homo viator. That is, he rejects the idea of a wispy ideal of infinite progress of intellect, upon which Schiller has seized in
recognizing the dilemma in that Kantian dualism to which
Schiller nevertheless remains committed. In the 1930s, Gilson
addresses this intellectual dead-end of idealism in several
essays, only recently collected under the title *Methodical
Realism* (1990). A passage or two from those essays will

clarify the perspective we shall take in considering Schiller and Tolstoy as representative of the ill effects of this new idealism upon the poet, out of Cartesian idealism and Kantian universalism as escape from complex creation itself.

In countering the Cartesian dislocations of consciousness from existential reality – from the immediacy of actual present experiences of an actual creation, through which consciousness journeys seeking its proper end – Gilson engages the Cartesian formulation underlying the new idealism which has been made popular in our own century. That is, Cartesian idealism becomes the dominant thematic matter to art itself, centering upon the "self," in self-heroics of alienation, flirting with the myth of the "Abyss." By that adoption, the poet easily supposes himself justified in a subjectivism whose disturbing effect upon actual community has been an alienation of selves from any prospect of community as faring in a continuous body through the variousness of creation itself. Gilson, contrary to Descartes, insists that *"Res sunt, ergo cognosce, ergo sum res cognoscens."* Given the triumph of Modernist metaphysics out of Cartesian origins, Gilson's formulation is a revolutionary pronouncement, disturbing to the comfortable authority presumed by Modernism, a doctrine in which the most treasured principle is that man's intellect is autonomous. For the Modernist position must maintain intellect to be the ultimate authority in questions of truth, beauty, good. Against that position, Gilson is insistent in his reformulation of Descartes: "Things exist; therefore I know; therefore I am a knowing subject." Thus he points to the supposed omnipotence of subjectivism as pronounced by intellectual autonomy as self-evidently dependent upon prior conditions to its own existence, despite its denials of dependence. Gilson's argument is made, of course, from his own initial dependence upon common sense, the ground to intellect out of which philosophy itself rises, as both he and Maritain will insist along the way in their several arguments. Theirs is an insistence learned of Thomas Aquinas, for whom the growing sophistication of common sense is first fed by the realities of the senses themselves in response to actual existence of things encountered through the body's senses, rationalized under the guidance of natural law. That is the fundamental point of departure for Thomas, whose whole visionary accommodation is to the *limits* of his own existence. It is out of this ground that he holds an inviolable truth: man is *intellectual soul incarnate*. Thus intellectual autonomy as a principle is a most destructive violation of the given nature of the *person* – of man.

Gilson concludes from his reformulation of Descartes' *cogito ergo sum* that a distinction is necessary in response to the circumstances of an intellectual distortion of reality by Modernist dreams of intellect as itself omnipotent. The distinction he insists upon is between the *idealist* out of Descartes and the *realist* as understood by Thomas Aquinas. "What distinguishes the realist from the idealist," he says, "is not that the one [the realist] refuses to undertake [an analysis of the nature of intellect in relation to its self-awareness] whereas the other [the idealist] is willing to, but that the realist refuses to take the final term of his analysis [*I am a knowing subject*] for a principle generating the thing being analyzed," namely the self-conscious "I" as an end which is also its own beginning. He adds that, "Idealism derives its whole strength from the consistency with which it develops the consequences of its initial error."

And thus, in consequence of that error, Cartesian idealism finds that "the order and connection of ideas replaces the order and connection between things [as they actually exist]. . . . Idealism can justify everything with its method except idealism itself." To the contrary, Realism "starts with an acknowledgment by the intellect that it will remain dependent on [an *a priori*] reality which causes its knowledge. Idealism owes its origin to the impatience of reason which wants to reduce reality to knowledge so as to be sure that its knowledge . . . lets none of reality escape." What lies ahead for such an intention is a totalitarian office to intellect as the lord absolute over existential reality through its knowledge.

That is a terrifying aspect of idealism all too familiar in our century in manifestations of power we characterize as ideologies.

Out of this intentionality, sprung from idealistic reason, then, illusion will follow, especially that illusion whereby ideas replace reality itself as the only reality agreeable to intellect – a deportment of intellect which can only dislocate it and distance it from actual reality. Thus the illusion grows that intellect through reason creates reality. That action of intellect is believed to determine absolutely the truth of created things. There follows from Descartes down to us a seductive rationale to this presumption made persuasive by Kant. Kant enlarges upon the primary role of idea as ultimately independent of reality. He is less concerned perhaps that "some of reality escape" the control of knowledge than he is dedicated to a formulation and constellation of ideas as intellect's escape from the impurities of reality. Thus an illusion of a constellation of ideas is projected, which by virtue of their consistency within that projected arena of ideas is argued to lie beyond the erosions of reality. That is the only consistency Kant sees possible to intellect's consent. And so that realm of a consistent illusion – unified ideas – becomes for Kant the highest reach possible to intellect, a reach attainable to the philosopher. That is Kant's solution to a threatening isolation of consciousness in the Cartesian closed circle of the self which Gilson rejects. It is, indeed, a species of angelism which Kant bequeaths us.

The pathos in Kantian philosophy, haunting all departments of our attempts at community and especially haunting our art through Kant's influence, is an effect of the separation of intellect itself from existential reality – a separation from "nature" in our popular designation of that reality. It is an inevitable pathos because the Kantian version of idealism, misnamed "transcendentalism" (note his influence on our New England men of letters in the 19th century) has as its motive a transcendence of "nature," through an energy derived intellectually by *immanent* intellect. But in the end intellect must account for itself in its origins as out of existential reality, out of "nature." By avoiding that necessity, pathos settles upon intellect. That is why neither Cartesian nor Kantian idealism can account for itself through its own terms of illusion, as Gilson and Maritain will argue. And that is why as well it is improperly called a "transcendental" philosophy. It is rather, once more, an angelism pretending to a transcendentalism.

Alas, intellect, in this perspective, continues undeniably mired in the swampy ground of existential reality despite denials, as Socrates observed and lamented long ago, recorded for us in Plato's pursuit of transcendental Idea, though Plato's idea more genuinely attempts transcendence than do Modernist versions. First, and closest "home" to intellect, is its own body, which for Tolstoy became the ultimate enemy. Intellectual soul *incarnate* – there lies the problem, as Socrates observes. In our Modernist concerns for an ultimate Idealism created by immanent intellect, the pathos of dissociation from the immanent proves overwhelming, leading us into a dead end of the "self" and of "community" at our juncture of history. It is an experience of reality which gives rise to our epitaph for our age: the "Age of Alienation." And so we see in Schiller and Tolstoy a poignant, if sometimes also irritating, attempt at a philosophy of art whereby they would rescue art, and thus the alienated consciousness, from the clutches of "nature."

In our concerns for the poignancy of these poets' isolation, often arrogantly enlarged out of their desperation and full of prophecy of utopian reconciliation of alienated selves in some divine, far-off brotherhood through art, we shall take recourse direct and sometimes implicit to Thomistic realists such as Gilson and Maritain, then. We shall, for instance, call to service Jacques Maritain's incisive critique of Kant, specifically that which he makes in his *Introduction to the Basic Problems of Moral Philosophy* (1950, tr. 1990). Not only incisive, but often angry, Maritain is thus the more intense in his concern as a response to absurdities out of recent philosophy (Descartes and Kant in particular). He sees each as having destructively disoriented social and political life in this century, affecting our art, particularly in art's relation to the chaos of the *polis*. By that Modernist address to art, art itself tends to become both a cause and an effect to the disintegration of community as now lamented by almost everyone.

What we might conclude, concerning the wider disintegration of community is that the philosopher, increasingly confident of intellectual autonomy, turns increasingly to the Absurd as his pseudo-Platonic Idea, exacerbating the alienation of persons within community. Such poet fathers as Schiller and Tolstoy resist intuitively, "feeling" an importance of community, to be rescued by the agency of the poet. What they contributed, however, proved but a further exacerbation of a false freedom already posited by Modernism. They, too, at last rest faith in autonomous intellect, to intellect as becoming in its operation less and less beholden to the actualities of nature and of human nature. That is the climate of Modernist thought to which they also contribute, a climate still dominant at the close of the 20th century. Into that poisonous climate to intellect we must enter, with Gilson and Maritain – and especially with Thomas Aquinas – to do battle with the gnostic lords of an intentional power over being itself. We consider Schiller and Tolstoy, then, as important poets, in part because they influence subsequent poets but more important to our concern because their influence is detrimental to the concerns of community. They argue art from positions insufficiently grounded in the reality of human nature. As representative of Western and Eastern Romanticism, then, we shall remark them as they engage the mystery of beauty under Kantian influence. But as we turn to our engagement of their arguments, a preliminary suggestion of our own perspective.

Ours is, to borrow from a popular concern for the conditions to our incarnate existence in the world, an "environmental" issue, whose concern is to reclaim the intellectual air which we must all breathe by virtue of our given nature as intellectual creatures. That involves us in the larger and inclusive war underway in the intellectual arena which must also include science and politics, though in the pages to follow we shall somewhat limit our own actions to a limited sector of that war: that designated as the battle over art. Whatever sector within the larger war, however, we shall always discover as the potential casualty and sacrifice intellect itself – whether intellect be engaged in politics or science or art. The rescue of intellect, then, becomes a concern always to be pursued, according to whatever gifts, in whatever local (and so seemingly limited) battle. The cumulative issue of course is the sacrifice or rescue of the person: *homo viator; person* as *intellectual soul incarnate on his always tenuous way.*

Friedrich Schiller
as Kantian Romantic

i

Both Kant and Schiller are dualists, the one intending to anneal dualism by philosophy, the other by art. Each would resolve the philosophical difficulty of Plato's One-and-Many dilemma, but neither sees that possible at last unless he can assume that intellect is autonomous. By assuming autonomy, a sufficient authority may be presumed whereby he may unify – anneal – duality itself, resolving duality by a willed autonomous unity of intellect through intentionality. For Schiller, the annealing faculty is the imagination whose instrument is art. For Kant, reason's categories serve the necessity. In Schiller's perspective, the poet is (as he would have it) superior to both the philosopher (including his contemporary mentor Kant) and the scientist (the latter trapped by a materialistic machine called "nature" as it appears to Schiller). As for Schiller, intellectual categories are to be dissolved through intellectual sovereignty. The provinces of science, theology, philosophy are thus to be made subject to poetry. His is a position with which we are more immediately familiar, perhaps, in Shelley, signaled in his famous declaration that the poet is the unacknowledged legislator of mankind. And Shelley means the poet as legislator dominant in theology, philosophy, and science no less than in politics.

As Schiller would have it, by art one discovers "the individual himself becoming the state," and man in time being *"ennobled to the stature* of man as idea." He insists upon the point in his "Fourth Letter" of *Letters on the Aesthetic Education of Man* (1795). If the state exists as representative of that "ideal man, the archetype of a human being," it is so as objectified by man's will, in a projection of the "ideal man." Meanwhile, the ideal man "is to be discerned more or less clearly in every individual." Nevertheless, the state as so projected must not "encroach upon this sovereign right of [each] personality...."

The end to which this confused thought must lead is that *each* personality must be conceded as sovereign, must come to be accepted each as his own state, making community thereby problematic. But if such were accomplished, a chaos of anarchic sovereignties must constitute the political state, since there is no authority beyond personality. The teleological flaw in Schiller's argument pops to the surface of his argument in Letter Five: Ideal man can only be found in "honoring man ... as an end in himself," toward which end a program of progress is forecast. But progress lies in each man's establishing his own intention as the dominant necessity to the end. It is a necessity, however, which can only be "created" by the artist. Ideal man, therefore, is the specific personality become perfected as artist.

In Letter Nine, Schiller addresses this programming of the self through art as imperative to self-perfection. The artist responds to "the divine impulse to form" which "often hurls itself directly upon present-day reality and upon the life of action [counter to it], and undertakes to fashion anew the formless material presented by the moral world." That "formless material" is the *all* we call *nature*, including that present "nature" called the spirit of the age. And that wayward spirit must especially be refashioned by the moral imperative of beauty as the ultimate heaven to the ideal man as artist. It is thus that the artist exploits the "pure moral impulse" by directing that impulse "towards the absolute," that is, toward beauty. For the artist, then, "the eyes of reason that knows no limits" discovers a magic transformation in himself. The "direction is at once the destination, and the way is completed from the moment it is trodden." This is Schiller's magic, presented as mystery, whereby through pure intention to beauty the artist accomplishes a self-perfection. The means is an intention to the beautiful, a direction "toward the absolute" called beauty. The magic lies in a means transformed into the ultimate end without any causal agency beyond the intentionality of the sovereign self.

We have heard this argument before, and in a spokesman for this rational justification of art's gnostic ends. Closer to us in time, James Joyce's young artist Stephen Dedalus argues much the same. Some irony, then, in Schiller's address in this Letter (Nine) to "the young friend of truth and beauty." That young friend as artist must by intentionality to beauty "satisfy the noble impulses of his heart." He must do so in this manner: "in the modest sanctuary of your heart . . . you must rear victorious truth, and project it out of yourself in the form of beauty, so that not only thought can pay it homage, but sense, too, lay loving hold on its appearance." Thus "sensibilities" are reunified as the artist becomes the ideal man. It appears to Schiller, however, as a possible end only for Schiller, who as perfect artist refuses to be drawn into the present world by his failed fellowmen. He must as perfect artist become the suffering savior in expiation of their failure. Joyce's Stephen Dedalus is less naive than Schiller in this respect, knowing that by his own intentionality he is choosing Satan's Word: *Non servium*. "I will not serve that in which I no longer believe, whether it call itself my home, my fatherland, or my church: and I will try to express myself in some mode of life or art as freely as I can and as wholly as I can, using for my defense the only arms I allow myself to use – silence, exile, and cunning."

Thus Stephen to Cranly in farewell, whereupon he is left to speak only to himself in increasingly fragmented notes that conclude Joyce's *Portrait of the Artist as a Young Man*. To encourage himself on setting out from Dublin he affirms:

"Welcome, O life! I go to encounter for the millionth time the reality of experience and to forge in the smithy of my soul the uncreated conscience of my race." Stephen's *soul* and Schiller's *heart* mean much the same, Stephen having rejected the traditional concept of the soul and appropriated the term to his own reductionist uses. (Schiller doesn't mention the term *soul*.) In the sanctuary of the heart, Stephen sets up his forge, fired by intentionality, to make a truth which is as yet nonexistent, "uncreated," until he turns his artist's hand to it. Thus is "truth" reared victorious over all, declared into existence by art itself. That is the final end toward which Schiller's principles lead, his argument reeking of the pathetic in that he supposes that by his principles he can establish the truth of "ideal man" through the magic of beauty, the only grace he allows to creation – either to man or to nature. For Schiller, the first and "fundamental law" to be engaged is "of mixed nature," whereby material and spiritual aspects of that nature are embroiled till art molds them into beauty. What isn't addressed (by Kant sufficiently nor by his disciple Schiller in his formulation) is the antecedent – the question of the implied but ignored "mixer" whereby nature may be said to be mixed *before* intellect's engagement of it. What is primary in respect to nature, from Schiller's initial engagement of it, is only a "physical necessity," in which is already implicit an acceptance of the material universe as accidental. In his *On the Sublime* and *On the Pathetic*, he engages "fundamental laws" whose judgmental execution is the providence of the poet: "*first*: depiction of suffering nature; *second*: depiction of moral independence in [by means of] suffering."

As in retrospection we engage the growing rationalistic position of the Enlightenment, by which the conclusion that intellect is an autonomous presence within the closed materialistic, mechanistic world, we may discover this new emerging faith raising inevitable questions beyond its sense of sure answers about existential reality. We may also suspect such a "Romantic" poet as Schiller of appropriating the concepts of a rationalistic view of the universe as both closed and deter-

mined. He would have it the province of the poet, who is at
war with science, the most conspicuous partisan of rationalistic
autonomy. What Schiller attempts as artist and rationalizer of
the authority of the artist is to command that Enlightenment
perspective, so largely held by science, through a theory of
the imagination as capable of transcending such mechanistic
entrapments. He would have it so on the authority of intentional uses of the imagination. And in forcing that argument,
he avoids for a little while those questions about the new
rationalism that is reaching climactic confusions of thought in
the late nineteenth century, played out on the world's stage in
the social and political dramas anticipating the greater bloody
chaos of our own century as that earlier century's denoue-
ment.

In a deference to residual sentiments lingering under the
influence of Christianity (a presence in history he carefully
avoids acknowledging), Schiller declares as necessary to
imagination's salvific offices the artist's vision of "nature"
itself as "suffering." He adds to this perspective the moral
imperative of intellect's "independence in suffering" – its
willed acceptance of its own suffering as savior artist.
Sufferings coordinated by imagination effect the rescue of
both nature and man, though from what vile agency the suffering descends is left in suspense. We might summon out of
the second half of the nineteenth century the vision of another poet concerned with suffering, another of the sons of Kant,
initially disoriented by Kantian thought, but an artist who
must at last face the questions avoided by Schiller in the
unfolding of Kantian philosophy. Dostoyevsky is frustrated
by that (to him) diabolical Enlightenment thought which at
first appears made intellectually serene by Kant, and so made
infectious of the Russian intelligentsia. He sees in the political
and social turmoil rising in his beloved Russia a Nihilism as a
new religion both anticipating and later following upon the
brutal adumbration of that thought we discover in Nietzsche.
And so with Dostoyevsky we might be given pause, ours the
advantage of hindsight across the wounded body of humani-

ty and nature from our vantage point at our century's turning. Thus, in relation to Schiller's generalized, even sentimental, attribution of "suffering" to nature and his election of intellect's "independence in suffering" as distinct from nature's suffering, Dostoyevsky reacts to that unfolding of Kantian ideas through traumatic and violent actions of imaginative opposition in his fiction. For a Kantian dualism both haunts and distorts the mystery of suffering for this Russian. Dostoyevsky engages the mystery of suffering as that mystery has become confused by recent Western philosophy in fiction after fiction from his *Notes from Underground* to *The Brothers Karamazov*. And he engages suffering in notes and letters to his life's end. But for him it has become Christ's suffering that is central.[1]

Schiller's appropriations and modifications of Kantian rationalism underlines for us not only our intellectual but our spiritual perils as well, most immediate to us out of Kant's concern for "pure" reason independent of both nature and the transnatural, except as rational intellect may establish itself as transnatural in being dissolved into the universal. And Kant as a father of modern idealism has affected decisively much of our literature, beginning with Schiller. He does so increasingly as we may notice in the poet's reaction to the growing authority of mechanistic science as the ultimate measure of man. If he contributes to intellect's disorientation, he nevertheless signals a necessity of reaction to mechanistic reductions of existence which insist that the universe is only a

---

1   In contrast to which, consider the extrapolation of this suffering out of dualism by those strange Kantians who now issue as New Age folk. In Theosophy, suffering becomes thematically central, but not in relation to a recovery of nature through grace but in a rejection of nature in a Manichean adaptation of Eastern mysticism, particularly of Hinduism and Buddhism. The movement known as Theosopy, now in a revival, shows this. See Peter Washington's careful "History of the Mystics, Mediums, and Misfits" who evolve Spiritualism in our century, in a book called *Madame Blavatsky's Baboon: AHistory of the Mystics, Mediums, and Misfits Who Brought Spiritualism to America*, Schoken Books, 1995.

machine. But there prove formidable dangers in Kant which
the poet has not escaped. If he opposes existence as merely
mechanistic, Kant in his "universals" implies at last a closed
cosmos. (On this weakness in him, again, see Jacques
Maritain's *Introduction to the Basic Problems of Moral
Philosophy*, 1950, Kant the major antagonist in this work.)

Given a closed universe, the refuge of the spiritual lies in
immanence, the transcendent having been directly rejected or
denied by implication. The idealism that evolves, then, finds
its ultimate ground in human consciousness, and in this
respect the human mind is assumed to bear in itself an
instinct for a perfection of consciousness. What the ends of
such a perfection implies, given a closed universe, can only be
at most some species of immanent humanism. The point, put
in summary, is seen in Friedrich Schiller's argument (belief,
faith?) in a proposition: "The destiny of man," he says, is "to
be God's peer." Further, "Eternity is the measure of infinity. In
other words, the spirit will develop infinitely but will never
attain its ideal." In this belief lies planted the signal effect
upon Romantic art by Schiller. Art so taken can never truly
rise beyond pathos into either a tragedy or comedy.

Nevertheless, given the ruthless dominance of reason
tuned to the rationalistic faith in the universe as accidental
machine, the poet resists through a Kantian idealism, whose
philosophical origin (we remember) is in Descartes. Descartes
attempt to rescue spirit is through reason, mathematics his
most steadying metaphysics. That failing, Schiller elects the
imagination seated in the heart, not the head. By the close of
the 19th century, the poet – the Romantic poet – found himself in desperate circumstances, given the emerging triumph
of the concept of random accident as the first and continuing
cause of particularly existing things in the triumph of reason
as science. And so what a late welcomed rescue to the poet,
then, Henri Bergson's *Creative Evolution*, his concept of the
élan vital immanent in mechanistic "nature." Therefore by
imaginative action, man could be rescued from sheer mecha-

nism through intellect itself. It is an imaginative argument
that will lead Bergson himself to declare that "the universe is
a machine with which to make God." The maker of God in
this perspective can only be man himself.

Bergson was an immediate influence on our poets, particularly in the West. Robert Frost, T. S. Eliot, Ezra Pound, and
William Carlos Williams were affected. Pound's Imagism and
Vorticism are out of Bergson. (Eliot found Bergson a dead
end.) And Bergson influenced philosophical thought as well –
Jacques Maritain and Eric Voegelin were among his early
respondents. But in the issue Voegelin and Maritain and Eliot
discover inadequacies. Maritain traces the problematic back
to Kant. Meanwhile, Kantian Idealism continues to have its
way with many of our poets. And Tolstoy never recovers, at
last seeking a Manichaean solution, unconvinced as is Schiller
that art can heal the body-spirit breach which is the burden of
Kantian idealism. Even so Tolstoy cannot refrain from the sinfulness of writing stories. Closer to home, Kantian idealism is
held by John Crowe Ransom, and his persistence drives him
apart from his peer-friends, Allen Tate, Donald Davidson, and
Andrew Lytle. Apart even from that sad Romantic poet
Robert Penn Warren, who can neither accept nor effectively
reject the immanent entrapment of Modernist thought in
rationalistic, materialistic, mechanistic aspects of our science.
Nor can Warren find refuge in the too-easy romanticism of the
idealist struggling to make God out of nature as in the train of
our Romantic poets still with us.

ii

Schiller is, then, in the light of Eric Voegelin's analysis of
Modernism, a gnostic who as poet would reconstitute existential reality by intentional acts of the imagination declared
to be out of sufferings made for failed creation. There is in
him the seed of that Sartrean Existential principle whereby
man is not created but makes himself and by that making

becomes thereby the only God. That this is so is spoken to in Schiller's *On the Aesthetic Education of Man*. There are, says Schiller in Letter Eleven, "two fundamental laws of sensuo-rational nature" (i.e., the nature of that creature called man). The first "insists upon absolute reality." Now that insistence requires an action, whereby man must "turn everything that is mere form into [a part of] the world, and make all his potentialities fully manifest." That second fundamental law "insists upon absolute *formality*." Thus it requires of man that he "eradicate everything in himself which is merely [part of the] world and bring harmony into all his changes; in other words he is to externalize all that is within him, and give form to all that is outside him." By such action man accomplishes his own perfection. For thus he neutralizes the dualism of his circumstances, and behold – the "concept of divinity" is revealed. It is the "ideal of human nature" accomplished as an action preceding being.

As for Schiller as modern gnostic, we need only remember his words in a letter to Goethe (September 14, 1797): "Two things have to be part of the poet and artist: that he lifts himself above reality and that he remains within the sensuous realm. Where these two are joined, there is aesthetic art." Art is man's act of grace in rescuing himself and thereby nature through an imaginative angelism, an act possible only to the artist through his profound commitment to his consciousness as independently autonomous, self-created. Schiller's vision of the poet, then, is out of Kantian "transcendentalism." But Kant's is not truly transcendent, being rather a sub-species of intellectual angelism. For Schiller this is an idealization whereby man believes himself removed from nature to a degree that he may then exercise control over nature, a control more comfortably called "suffering." If Thomas Aquinas holds the existing thing as a simple unity effected through the act of creation – form and substance separated only speculatively – for Kant there is an insistent duality without which he could not exercise his angelism. The Adam of the self must be split. His perfection is of idea – of concept as in the control of the extra-consciousness of the philosopher rather than the poet. In idea alone lies the possibility of a simple unity, but it is the simple unity of a Cartesian isolation, despite such high terms as transcendentalism. It is this Kantian dualism that Schiller would correct, but in a Kantian manner. The poet supersedes the philosopher.

By will, Kant would have intellect occupy a realm beyond the reach of nature, and therefore beyond the reach of mere science, the emerging threat to both philosopher and poet. In the country of mind which he imagines, intellect begets progeny to be reconciled in a community, but not a community of persons. It is a determined community of ideas, determined by his will. These are ideas spawned by "pure reason." Thus it is not God, but the *idea* of God sprung from Kant which is declared the first cause of these supra-natural existences, ideas. By ironic reflection, we must conclude (as Maritain does) that Kant's intellect must be deduced as the first cause of this supra-natural country in Kantian metaphysics, wherein imperatives metamorphose from natural instinct into a moral relevance.

Kant is open to us in this matter, justifying imperatives as derived from natural causes, to be deployed out of transcendent necessities to intellect. Thus he addresses his ultimate reality as illusional, as a projection by intellect out of its ultimately unaccountable necessity for a sense of unity. It is seen by Kant as an illusional projection, but acceptable to him as ultimate since thereby intellect may by illusion extend and order *ideas* – those creatures of the projecting mind, made acceptable because made non-contradictory by an inner intellectualized consistency in the willed projection. By "pure" reason's deployment of idea as ultimate, then, duality is to be overthrown. Thus, as the editors of Schiller's *Essays*, Walter Hinderer and Daniel O. Dahlstrom, say in a note of their introduction, Kant's celebrated *Critique of Pure Reason* might better be parsed as a "critique of the ideas of pure reason."

Within that purified realm, which is removed from nature itself and all of nature's messy and contradictory complexities, there can be made to appear no contradiction *within* the projected ideas. It is in a sense an action of an entrapped philosopher made through poetry, through an imaginative leap. What one has, then, is Plato's vision of the transcendent idea, which is truly transcendent for Plato, relocated by Kant: the realm of the ideal as absolute is located *in* man's own intellect as a fiction called transcendentalism. Kant's vision is an inverted Platonism. But by that inversion we discover subsequent effects in nature – in community and family in particular. They are most disturbingly evident at the close of our own century two hundred years after Kant as philosopher and Schiller as Kantian poet.[2]

iii

What is underway in Schiller's "Letters on the Aesthetic Education of Man," especially in "Letter Eleven" and the next few, is Schiller's confused attempt at a metaphysics justifying an *idea of human nature*, not human nature as a reality. As if he were a new Dante, having experienced and been absorbed by the transcendental idea himself, he makes the attempt. The central agency to his metaphysics is an intentionality within human nature which is never clarified. The argument depends on the Kantian conclusion of idea as a transcendent sufficiency to intellect, but the argument circles in that man

---

2   Not unexpectedly, each Kantian intellect must be itself ultimate intellect. Schiller puts this necessity in a letter (Nov. 4, 1795): "The highest philosophy ends in a poetic idea, so do the highest morality and the highest politics. It is the poetic spirit that indicates the ideal to all three, and to approach it is their greatest perfection." On that approach the "they" will find the poet already comfortably settled. Thus a revenge against Plato's dream of the philosopher king and perhaps against Machiavelli's political Prince, the Poet having been enthroned by Schiller as the king of idea. For Schiller, then, as he says in his Ninth Letter, "Truth lives on in the illusion of art."

must himself create that idea. There is, then, a polarity of suspension between idea and consciousness itself, and that is not only a closed "world," but a world closed against nature, both human nature *per se* and actual creation as we perceive it. Not that Schiller fails to recognize a dilemma here, for he spends considerable argument on yet another closed world contingent on that suspension of consciousness and transcendent idea within abstract idea itself. That is, he argues a dual nature in man: that between "person" and the world of the "senses." The initiating cause of this conglomerate ignored – i.e., the First Cause – is not his concern, however. For what he is about is substituting man for God at last. Let us pursue this substitution.

Schiller is concerned with a "maximum autonomy and maximum intensity" to consciousness, to be achieved by an intentionality which at once both posits that fulfillment and is agent of that fulfillment. But is this merely an "instinctive" agent to potentiality? What he must deny is teleology to the existing man, empowered by intentionality to formal decress. Thus he may justify his assertion that "the direction is at once the destination." Thus he denies any teleological end independent of intentionality, a denial possible only through art as totalitarian over mind. Art is sufficient, in that "Truth lives on in the illusion of art." Thus "the nobility of art *survived* the nobility of nature" as an "afterimage" which implicitly and confusingly is magically "foreimage" as well. It is so in that an intentional projection of idea is the art act whereby nature can be said to exist as a "world" counter to "person." In pursuit of this fulfillment there comes to be a necessity of beauty in art. But it is a "pure *rational concept* of beauty . . . since it cannot be derived from any actual case, but rather itself corrects and regulates our judgment of every actual case."

This beauty is "to be discovered by a process of abstraction, and deduced from the sheer potentialities of our sensuo-rational nature." That is a difficult role for beauty, but even more difficult to thought is the necessity to *abstract* and *deduce*. Therefore "we must lift our thoughts to the pure concept of human nature. . . . True, this transcendental way will lead us out of the familiar circle of phenomenal existence, away from the living presence of things, and cause us to tarry for a while upon the barren and naked land of abstractions. But we are, after all, struggling for a firm basis of knowledge that nothing shall shake. And he who never ventures beyond actuality will never win the prize of truth." Thus the poet as Kantian.

The strategy is justified for Schiller since we as man are "the absolute subject" of the attempt. Only in the absolute subject alone "do all its determining attributes persist *with* the personality, since all of them proceed *from* the personality. What the Godhead is, and all that it is, it is just *because* it is." Thus the supersession by man himself to the attributes traditionally given only to God. As for "personality" thus conceived, it "is consequently everything for all eternity, because it is eternal," made immortal (this is to say) through this intentional usurpation in the name of absolute freedom, absolute autonomy: a usurpation of Godhead. And so the teleological end of person is the beginning of person, the serpent of the self swallowing its own tail.

Schiller is capable of seeing this dead end, but only in relation to natural science, as is evident in one of his footnotes. Natural scientists move slowly because possessed "obviously [by] the universal, and almost uncontrollable, propensity to teleological judgments, in which, once they are used constitutively, the determining faculty is substituted for the receptive." It is only in the realm of *idea*, rather than of nature, that this procedure is to be justified – the teleological in respect to idea used constitutively as "the determining faculty" which is at once both "determining" and "receptive." Such is the process of self-making. It is a clever dodging of that barrage of bullets aimed at such speculative abstractionism by common sense understanding of the realities of this actual person's experiences of nature. For by experience common sense knows mind and nature included within some larger perspective independent of consciousness as "determining" truth, wherein is a determinate "faculty" independent of mind itself: a cause beyond the individual as ultimate causing agent. That admission by Schiller would, of course, mean the collapse of his house of cards, his speculative abstractionism reared by fancy in defiance of reality. In order to maintain this fancy by rhetorical art, he must require of us an acceptance of an illusion: the illusion that man is as individual a closed world, an all in all.

Out of a polar suspension of man between sensual and intellectual "natures" he posits this closed world, by a shell-game of Kantian rhetoric. Schiller attempts to persuade us, against our own experiences of existing as persons, that consciousness is a closed world, ideally so because autonomous. By an intellectual energy of reconciliation of form and matter within consciousness, a balance derived by the arcing of an energy of intentionality as if an electricity called life, he declares that man – thus balancing the polarity of himself – is transformed and transported into an ultimate light. The vision accomplished he calls, with his emphasis, *"the idea of his* [man's] *human nature."* Thus man achieves an autonomous absolute through the tensional "drives" – the "form drive" which has as its principle "moral constraint"; and the "sense drive" whose principle is the "physical," is "matter." In this balance achieved by intentionality, presumably under the auspices of will, man is "set . . . free both physically and morally." He thus transcends the contingencies of the actual and moves beyond that balance, within which little world the inclinations of person and sense are not only counter to each other through contingencies but threaten an abnormality in man when balance fails. Thus may result the abnormality of either an excess of the one or the other, an excess of the sensual "matter" or the intellectual "form." The transcendence beyond both physical and moral complications is a move into a Kantian-Nietzschean world of idea, in which man exists as Superbeing, man as God.

What is left hanging is the *will*, necessary to a balance and a subsequent transcendence. For will must be in this vision in operation as the agent to both the *person* and the *sensual*. (Schiller is careful to set aside *soul* and *body* as terms.) It must reconcile into a balance the "forces" – the *form drive* and the *sense drive*, in Schiller's terms. But whence comes will? Is it a moral agent *created* by person? Through thought? If so, it is a subordinate rather than the necessary superior agent required. Only on the supposition that man creates himself and is therefore God in his closed world – the made abstract country of idea – is such strange metaphysics possible. But that is exactly the line of argument in Schiller. For man, "only inasmuch as he is autonomous, is there reality outside him and he is receptive to it; and only inasmuch as he is receptive, is there reality within him and is he a thinking force." Thus man is "to seek absolute being by means of determinate being, and a determinate being by means of infinite being. He is to set up a world over against himself because he is a person, and he is to be person because a world stands over against him."

And behold, the ideal idea: "Should there . . . be cases in which he were to have this twofold experience *simultaneously*, in which he were to be at once conscious of his freedom [as autonomous form-drive] and sensible of his existence [as sense drive], at one and the same time, to feel himself matter and come to know himself as mind, then he would in such cases, and in such cases only, have a complete intuition of human nature, and the object that afforded him this vision would become for him a symbol of his *accomplished destiny* and, in consequence (since that is only to be attained in the totality of time), serve him as a manifestation of the infinite."

"[I]n *such cases only*": Schiller is concerned for any common sense objections to his utopian vision of man as autonomous creature – a deism of the self. Therefore he must argue a sort of infinite regression of *"accomplished destiny."* For that destiny is never to be achieved, as he insists again and again. By that insistence he would avoid the necessity of arguing for his own versions of utopian Five Year Plans toward perfection. Meanwhile, a confusion here: man at once "sets up" a world of the sensual as a counter, and then counters it as a person – a playing of illusion possible only in an abstract and illusional world (which Kant at least admits to be illusional): the world of transcendent idea, in which alone contradictions are to be reconciled through accepting consistency within an illusion. For Schiller, there emerges "man" as a closed world bearing a polarity. Man may thereby move in the illusional idea of an infinite progress of the self. The infinity, however, is that provided by an unachievable but desired balance, since "The sense drive excludes from its subject all autonomy and freedom; the form drive [based on autonomy and absolute freedom] excludes from its subject all dependence, all passivity." Only in moments of self-revelation, a "twofold experience *simultaneously*" as a substitute for that Revelation called the Incarnation, is man "set...free both physically and morally." One must assume that in that perfect balance man is transubstantiated into idea. In idea posited by this climate of Kantian "universalism," we bide by thought in the country of illusion. And so the ultimate fulfillment of man as idea means that man is illusion. The cost of illusional consistency is the abolition of man.

What consolation? Schiller thinks to have effected consolation in relation to a will to perfection which is admitted in advance as never to be achieved. There is scant rational accommodation of will to this process toward "transcendence" in his argument. As for moral feeling, he says, it requires only the declaration *"this shall be,"* an action of command which is equal to God's "let there be light." For by such fiat "individuality" "decides forever and aye," thereby experiencing "the greatest enlargement of being," albeit an enlargement never to be achieved. Thus "man has raised himself to *a unity of ideas* embracing the whole realm of phenomena. During this operation we are no longer in time; time, with its whole never-ending succession, is in us. We are no longer individuals; we are species. The judgment of all minds is expressed through our own, the choice of all hearts is represented by our action." We are self-made as Christ to our self, and as such, in an overplus of intentionality, we may also imagine our self as a rescue of all persons. Why should one read further in Schiller? Perhaps only to reveal in him a pervasive blight on thought, scattered in thought's climate and affecting Romanticism as a response to science's deadening assertion of existence (including that of the person) as accident of an accidental universe. Spores of Kantian ideas corruptive of the reality of personhood, if we once consent to water them with the tears of a careless desire, prove at last inadequate to sprout viable persons toward spiritual ends.

iv

Jacques Maritain, in his *Introduction to the Basic Problems of Moral Philosophy*, takes Kant as the source of our modernist confusions of morality. He is the source, says Maritain, of "acosmic-idealist" confusions, confusions we find popularized out of German Romanticism. He is as well of those who "reject any kind of normative ethical system," in favor of ethics established "on the model of the natural sciences," being neither a system of the "cosmic-realist nor acosmic-realist." (Maritain's terms of distinction.) This species is "sociologism, which first developed in France" and spread from there out of Comte. In the evolution of Kantian moral philosophy there developed also a species of morality "grounded on a philosophy of nature" eschewing metaphysics, one species of which philosophy is Pragmatism, as supplying modes of process to Positivism. It is in response to this scientific imposition of an acosmic-idealism that Bergson makes a counter attempt, an attempt to ground ethics on "both a philosophy of nature and on a knowledge of absolute first realities." Thus Maritain's observation of Bergson's attempt written between the World Wars, his *Two Sources of Morality and Religion*.

Since Kant's position (says Maritain) is that of the "acosmic" idealist, his address to Christianity proves a perversion at last of Christian moral philosophy. It is so in that Kant attempts to transpose "revealed morality – into the framework and 'limits' of pure reason," thus excluding any supernatural dimension relevant to moral conduct. By insisting on a *disinterestedness* in addressing the problem as the proper deportment of the philosopher, Kant effectively "cut off" reason "from the real and from nature," content to settle for "an ethics of pure duty," divorced from any final end of moral conduct in the world – however high such a term as his *transcendentalism* may appear to subsequent disoriented idealists. For the ideal transcendence achieved as the perfected moral deportment of intellect through pure reason is a conduct of "disinterest" avoiding a truly moral commitment. Alas, between *disinterest* and simple *indifference* it is most difficult to establish a dependable distinction in the affairs of community itself. That this is so becomes evident in the Kantian morality which is evolved, on exhibit in German Idealism, one of whose philosophers proves to be Nietzsche. It is comically evident in the history of spiritualism as evolved out of Kant, as we have noted in such agents as Madame Blavatsky, a committed Kantian initially. It is out of Kant that she evolves Theosophy with its early amalgam of Masonic and Rosicrucian mythology, to which she adds Buddhist and Hindu elements in often spectacular attempts to find a way out of the closure of Kantian transcendentalism.

Maritain emphasizes this hidden danger in Kantian thought. It is the "process of immanentization which has developed over the course of modern times." Not that Kant is an absolute first cause, of course. For instance, Maritain cites

Luther's contribution in making irreducible opposites of the law and faith. But with the decline of theology, Kant as *disinterested* philosopher gains a general intellectual consent from the Modernist intellect not granted to the theologian. Through pure reason, then, consciousness perfects itself in act when it declares its independence of universal law, if it can but avoid at last that severe reaction out of such isolating independence – the reaction of an overwhelming despair. It is an act Kant holds to be supremely moral, he says, "when it is done without interest or motivation." That is, it is an act which must be untrammeled by personal cause, having been purified of any anticipation of personal end. For only thereby does it become an act "by a pure affirmation of freedom rising above the world of despair." How does such an act appear to mundane intellect? It is an act (again Maritain) characterized by "sincerity," so that inevitably "sincerity" becomes the "supreme measure of morality." Sincerity speaks a Kantian "transcendentalism" in which one's actions in the world are inevitably to be removed from consequences of actions in that world. What this means appears in bitterly comic abundance in that history of Spiritualism already alluded to, in which Peter Washington (in his *Madame Blavatsky's Baboon*) traces the influences of Theosophy and Spiritualism down to our present "New Age" neo-paganisms. What is to be deduced is the influences upon our "new age" in consequence of a Kantian transcendentalism out of which (as Maritain says), "things in themselves cannot be grasped." For reality is beyond reach "in Kant's system." The conjured spirits in Theosophy, one might put it, have residence in Kantian transcendental universalism.

With the development of German Idealism out of Kant, there begins a struggle to escape the implicit dead end of a Kantian angelism which leaves intellect orbiting creation, neither in nor out of the world but increasingly unsettled by recognitions of its transcendentalism as but *pseudo*. By that entrapment – by intellect's attempting to remove itself from nature by "pure reason" but by that very attempt prevented any grasping of things in themselves – there becomes established a tensional suspension of intellect in which it finds itself still inhabitant of a closed world which is not related at last to any transcendent. That new idealism, whose principals include the dramatist Friedrich Schiller, the poet Hölderlin, the philosophers Hegel (all of them former seminarians of the same institute) and Fichte, finds itself required to reconcile Kantian abstractionism (given an inescapable worldly dimension as "universals" trapped in orbit) to the growing materialistic, mechanistic explication of nature certified by the empirical sciences. For these sciences, to which Darwin will presently appear an adequate "metaphysician," Kantian transcendentalism is an inadequate response. For, as a secularized "transcendentalism," Kantian metaphysics baits both Pragmatism and Positivism, which react out of strict empirical devotions to materialism. That is a point not missed by Schiller, who vigorously commands "reason" to his position. As for the response to Kantian transcendentalism from the perspective of the Thomist, Maritain remarks, "Universality is not of the essence of the norm, as Kant believed; it is a consequence of the norm's rationality." The fateful consequences of this failure in Kant becomes ramified through Comtean sociology at last, we suggest, affecting increasingly both the academy and the state in grotesqueries which appear – though often with rhetorical persuasiveness – as if the norm.

The Idealist's attempt to reach a Modernist version of the Aristotelian "golden mean," reconciling abstract "form" as a universal with concrete "matter" as palpable and inert, can only come to emphasize as the *cause* of any possible reconciliation the *mind* of man. That is a principle the Idealist seems forced to share at last with the Positivist. And so for either, man becomes his own god of creation. Nevertheless, there continues a disquiet in the Kantian Idealist unless he can reconcile his perspective with that of the empirical Positivist. He cannot deny the actuality of impinging reality upon him, though he cannot accept that impinging world as what the Positivist asserts of it – the All. (Even so, the ordinary citizens of Kant's Königsberg, observing Kant in their streets, seem to have decided he rejected the impingement of that little world upon him.) The transcendent rationally secularized: that becomes the attempt at satisfying a nagging desire in intellect for some rescue beyond an admission that intellect itself is but grown out of mechanistic materialism. Thus for the Kantian there seems reason conflicted by an unreasonable faith which is antipathetic to the limited arena of Positivistic materialism.

What we may consider in this conflict between Kantian transcendentalism and Positivistic materialism vesting cause in mechanistic immanence is the difficulty of a false dilemma to intellect – if considered from a Thomistic position. For there seems to have occurred since the late Middle Ages, and with progressive intellectual contentions in consequence, a logically pervasive separation of intellectual sensibilities, whereby what Thomas calls the simple unity of our intellect is willfully segmented. In the social arena (embracing the cultural and political aspects of community) the person as person becomes doubly crippled. There is a willful demeaning of intellectual unity whereby the will elects to serve either a rational or an intuitive intent. But on either hand, a further complication of this distortion, either by the Enlightenment "Rationalist" or by the 19th century "Romantic" intuitivist, justifies intellectual autonomy through faith in intellect as autonomous. We intend to speak of antipathies simplified here, to speak metaphorically, recognizing that we are unlikely to encounter any pure Rationalist or Romantic.

Tendencies through willful distortion of intellect in its simple unity, then, crippled intellectual persons increasingly engage in ideological combat. And by their very embattlement, they give rise to "movements" which ironically contribute to a common emerging religion more and more popularly embraced – the religion of *Progress*. If one examine in this perspective the Modernist religion, he may discover it confused by sentimentality on either hand, whether in the would-be pure Rationalist or the would-be pure "Romantic." No accident, then, such a title as Kant's *Critique of Pure Reason*, nor of his pursuit of a "Transition from Metaphysical Foundations of Natural Science to Physics" in attempting reconciliation of his transcendentalism to the increasingly insistent limiting of that concern by Positivistic arguments. In the ideological wars there emerges increasingly a devotion to *process* as promising an object desired. As Eric Voegelin observes (*Science, Politics & Gnosticism*) there grows the "building of systems" as "a gnostic form of reasoning" counter to philosophy, for philosophy springs "from the love of being." Systems project objects to be commanded through process, in Progress to whatever Utopian object willed by desire.

As for that admixture to intent of a sentimentality confounding both intuition and reason – confounding at its source, common sense – we might put it summarily: intuited humanitarian concerns reduced from Transcendent Cause (a reduction we here attribute to Kant as exemplum of that continuing Idealism) mingles with Hegelian-Marxist totalitarian reason in deconstructions of community itself as the body seen from the Thomistic perspective. Thus that *body* is reduced to *mechanism*, through vague terms such as *society* (metamorphosed to the *State* through Marx). Society must be justified as devoted to a common good when made perfect system, its mechanics of process perfected. That perfection is possible when the *individual* becomes a perfected cog in the machinery of society. And so that version of persons as *members* constituting a body as community as seen from the Thomist's perspective becomes mechanistically only *individuals* serving process in the name of Progress, whose end is perfect society.

Concerning any prospect of reunifying intellect in the person, recovering complementary modes of the rational and the intuitive, Schiller makes his own attempt. To do so, he declares that the poet is responsible for that task, through the exercise of the imagination. To that end he declares all men ideally artists in opposition to the Positivistic ideal of a dominant man as scientist. For Schiller's is a strategy which would reduce rationalism from preeminence. To the contrary, Hegel as rationalist philosopher will play thesis against antithesis with a severity of logical control over the imagination, deriving his own "golden mean" distinct from the classical Aristotelian mean, but as well allowing it a species of transcendentalism whose cause is his own intellect. Thus will emerge a law determinate of reality from rational intellect itself, a law to be progressively imposed upon both nature and man in the continuous unfolding of thesis-antithesis-synthesis. Logic sheered from the mystery of existence becomes the instrument used to establish a totalitarianism of intellect itself.

Let us suppose both Schiller and Hegel to be Romantics. We may thereby discover them jointly complementary in progressive effects upon the popular mind, though initially their influence appear diverse in the intellectual community, from within which the conjoined influences radiate downward into the popular spirit. From the position of the Thomistic realist, this case can be made, beginning with Thomas's epistemology, in which he declares our intellect gifted as a singularity by modal properties of response to creation. There is a mode of the intuitive and of the rational. (The rational he argues an *extension* of the intuitive.) From this perspective we might see a dissociation of those modes progressively underway in post-Renaissance thought, yielding a partial nature to intellect as if the partial were the intellect's whole nature. Insofar as common sense – still active, if but vaguely active, in the "popular mind" – responds to these separated sensibilities of intellect, that mind may well find itself attracted to both, out of an inherent desire proper to intellect for a perfection of its simple unity proper to intellectual action. What by its nature it would recover is a healthful reassociation from the logically perverse separations.[3] Meanwhile, of course, these seemingly diverse Romanticisms (that of the so-called *Rationalist* and the *Romantic*) would establish as unique its own intellectual authority based in a faith in its own autonomy. And so both contribute – contrary to the intentions of either – to the emergence of that consent to Progress as the highest claim upon the popular spirit.

Desire has nevertheless been reduced to a closed world, whatever shibboleths of Kantian transcendentalism may be invoked. One might even, as does Josef Pieper in works such as his *In Tune with the World: A Theory of Festivity,* discover a beginning amalgamation of the two "Romanticisms" in the spectacle of the French Revolution, and see it unfolding in Marxist states as a theology to the doctrine of Progress. And to this evolving of secular religion, we may discover in Eastern Communism a surreptitiously borrowed mysticism, made rhetorically persuasive when put in a humanitarian clothing. But that humanitarian bent must be reduced to the appetitive limits of humanity. Indeed, Tolstoy himself contributes significantly to a "humanitarianism" loudly proclaimed by Lenin. With world enough and time, we could explore this coincidence as thematic concern in the fiction of Walker Percy, especially in his last novel, *The Thanatos Syndrome.* It is Percy who gives epithet to our age as that of the Theorist-Consumer, an amalgamation of autonomous intellect as theorist and the popular spirit as consumer of products derived from theory.

---

3   The theme of two species of "Romanticism," the imaginative and the rationalistic, I have explored at length in *Romantic Confusions of the Good: Beauty as Truth, Truth Beauty* (1997) and *Concerning Intellectual Philandering: Poets and Philosophers, Priests and Politicians* (1998). In *Making: The Proper Habit of Our Being* (1999) I attempt to recover a "reassociation" of sensibilities, an ordinate relation of what T. S. Eliot called "thought and feeling."

We see Schiller attempting this reconciliation, whereby the office of angelism implicit in Kantian "metaphysics" is assumed by the poet. It is to be exercised through reason (in contrast, for instance, to Tolstoyean Romanticism exercised by feelings through a rejection of reason). Schiller as romantic poet is very keen on the role of reason, aware of the distance from reality occasioned by Kantian transcendentalism and the advantage of a "pure reason" to gain persuasive power to be deployed by imagination. Thus he says, in "Concerning the Sublime": "All of nature acts in a rational manner; the human prerogative is simply to act in a rational manner consciously and deliberately." What is the *place* of this act in relation to the natural world to be ordered by man? It is the place made by art, superior to nature but yet unbeholden to any transcendence other than man's own reason as the agency to a new angelism of the sublime. For only thus "is the sublime married to the beautiful and our sensitivity to both [thus] shaped in equal measure." We are then "complete citizens of nature, without on that account being its slaves, and without squandering our citizenship in the intelligible world." Thus here and now we participate in the "heaven" made by angelism. That marriage lies under the authority of the priestly concern of art itself. "[A]rt of this sort [as envisioned by Schiller] detaches all the contingent limitations from its object and also leaves the mind of the observer free because it imitates only the *appearance* and not the *actuality*." Oh, brave New Age world in the making!

Nature is thus taken at its surface, the reality of things *in themselves* rejected, a Kantian inevitability spoken of by Maritain in saying that, "things in themselves cannot be grasped in Kant's system." One is left, though Schiller denies it, with mere fancy as the true country of art, though he does add a telling word to his consecration of art: "since all the magic of the sublime and the beautiful lies only in the appearance and not in the content, art possesses all the advantages of nature without sharing its chains." Such is the freedom of a self-perfection through art, but admitted as a possible perfection to only the *few* by Schiller. That is, he argues a pure art as the elitist's province, attainable only by the *exceptional* person, not by the *hoi polloi* – the historical irony of which is that this theoretical position runs counter to the wide popularity of Schiller's own plays. If Hegel was much taken with Schiller's aesthetics, seeing analogies between his own arguments and those of this contemporary poet, with the advent of Marx Hegelian thought becomes quickly purged of the aesthetic, dooming the poet, who is central to the welfare of humanity for Schiller, to an exile. The Stalinist address to the uses of art and Stalin's treatment of the independent artist in the Gulag lies ahead of Schiller and Hegel and Marx, the way having been prepared by them.

A consequence of Kantian thought, then, is a seeming enlargement of the Cartesian closed world of the singular consciousness, though that enlargement becomes only the closed world of a collectivist consciousness, a circumstance troubling to various species of resurrected imminence of spirit in the enlarged arena of conflicting, orbiting spirits. There was, for instance as we noted, Bergson and his *élan vital*. There will be Jung and his Collective Unconscious. There will be a resurgence of Romanticism out of Ezra Pound in Imagism and Vorticism, adaptations of immanence to poetry beholden to Kant through Bergson and at last intruding into politics and religion. There will occur the wave of Spiritualism, with its attempt to split the veil through Schillerian "magic," to gain a communion with unnamable masters from the "beyond," masters who speak through seances and promise immortality through Eastern ideas of reincarnation in response to the anxious recognition of the arena of consciousness as closed from the transcendent. There will be Theosophy and Rudolph Steiner's Anthroposophy when he rejects Theosophy – Steiner's an attempt to regain the rigors of a Kantian disinterested philosophy which he had learned from Kant before he was seduced by Madame

Blavatsky's Theosophy. In breaking with Theosophy, Steiner establishes his Goetheanum in Switzerland to advance his doctrine of Anthroposophy, reviving Goethe and Fichte and Hegel. (Steiner, incidentally, was a prime influence on Owen Barfield, who brings something of Steiner's thought into that circle of Inklings at Oxford.)

And there were others in reaction to the Kantian closures made in the name of transcendentalism. At about the time the Maritains were beginning their Thomistic Circles, the time T. S. Eliot was publishing his *Waste Land*, Gurdjieff was establishing his own Institute for the Harmonious Development of Man in a chateau near Fontainebleau. Gurdjieff declared himself the resident master through whom alone the transcendent spirits would speak the "Way," a way possible only through the suffering of his disciples. Those who think of such recent cults as that of the Davideans as possible only through simplistic and semi-literate provincialism should review the history of Gurdjieff, who attracted many of our century's celebrated intellectuals, particularly from among the literati. A role of names involved from the periphery to the center of this amorphous spiritualism reveals G. B. Shaw, William Butler Yeats, A. R. Orage (editor of the influential *New Age*), Katherine Mansfield, Aldous Huxley, Hart Crane, Christopher Isherwood, W. H. Auden, Margaret Anderson and Jane Heap of the *Little Review*, Frieda Lawrence (unsuccessful in persuading D. H.). Frank Lloyd Wright's wife Olga was a devoted disciple of Gurdjieff, who was a welcomed guest at the Wright's. There were many, many others from among our artists and intellectuals, either sympathetic to the new spiritualism or actually heavily involved as disciples.

Here it is well to be reminded once more of the overlap already suggested, whereby this species of spiritualism, so attractive to the intelligentsia as a substitute religion, was accompanied very often by equally high dreams about Joseph Stalin as humanitarian, as one of the elect masters – a tran-

scendent person so to speak. Perhaps the overlap is less curious than at first we might suppose. For in attempting an
angelism of transcendence over nature, as we have Schiller
advocating through art, out of that same climate of Kantian
thought there arise both Marx and Nietzsche. The political
prince as Superman Savior is sibling of the poet as Superman.
And for both prince and poet, a diminution of existential reality through the will is supposed the means to a self-elevation
beyond good and evil. It is a supposition entering Russian
politics through Nihilism, as Dostoyevsky recognized. No
wonder that for Dostoyevsky the Western Romantic poet
(Byron a prototype) was a deceptive hero, pretending to an
intellect superior to the ordinary, to the common intellect. To
Dostoyevsky's horror, such figures were concluded justified
in operating beyond good and evil in the name of humanity.
Dostoyevsky gives us a haunting portrait of such an emerging "master" in his Raskolnikov of *Crime and Punishment*, a
novel much admired by Nietzsche, though Nietzsche would
surely disapprove of Raskolnikov's turning toward
Christianity at that novel's end.

And so, the philosophical line of Kantian dislocations of
intellect from reality flows down to us in a widening stream.
From Kant through that German Romanticism we see emerging in Schiller, Hegel, Hölderin, through the struggles of phe-
nomenology in Husserl, to Heidegger (who hearkens often to
Hölderin). And to a dead end at last in John-Paul Sartre. A
variety of tributaries along the way feed the slow erosion of
reality which in its actuality involves both material and spiritual man. (That is, if we affirm man as intellectual soul incarnate.) In that descent we find ourselves a dead or dying
swamp of "humanity" at our century's close. At the soggy
center of this dislocation lies the Modernist principle derived
from a faith in immanence in denial of transcendence, explicitly the principle of intellectual autonomy. Out of that principle derives a widening dissipation of gnostic intentions to
self-sovereignty, exhibited in art and politics, in the academy

and the state. Supposing the individual intellect sovereign, the perfection of that sovereign intent is argued to lie in the individual's own power to a self-perfection. In the issue, then, all save the self becomes mere object to be rendered, dissolved and reconstituted, to the service of that sovereign autonomous self, its collective political shibboleth at the moment the individual's "rights." We see this evident in two pronouncements sufficient to our concluding point, one from Friedrich Schiller, the other from Henri Bergson:

> Schiller: "The destiny of man [is] to be God's peer. . . . Man's ideal is infinite; but the spirit is eternal. Eternity is the measure of infinity. In other words, the spirit will develop infinitely but will never attain its ideal."

> Bergson: "The Universe is a machine for the making of God."

On Reading Tolstoy's
What Is Art?

i

Tolstoy says near the beginning of his *What Is Art?* that "In Russian, by the word *krasota* [beauty] we mean only that which is pleasing to the sight." The whole of his treatise, however, is aimed against a corruption of the Russian address to beauty borrowed from Western aesthetics, imported to Russian salons of Moscow and St. Petersburg beginning at the mid-nineteenth century. His initial engagement is in a rejection of aesthetic significance to the other senses in respect to art, holding (though one suspects reluctantly holding) an older limit to beauty as related to human senses. (The root meaning of *aesthetics* is *sense perception*.) One suspects as much, given his companion treatises on man's unhappy circumstances in creation: *A Confession* (1879), *What I Believe* (1884), *What Is Religion and of What Does Its Essence Consist?* (1902). He labors at his treatise on aesthetics for a decade, his final version released in 1897. In relation to the fierceness of Tolstoy on the question of art in his diary, Henri Troyat remarks in his *Tolstoy* that this final version "is actually relatively mild," citing a passage in the diary of the author of *Anna Karenina* dated July 19, 1896: "Novels and short stories describe the revolting manner in which two creatures become infatuated with each other; poems explain and glorify how to die of boredom; and music does the same. And all the while life . . . is beating at us with urgent questions – food, the distribution of property, labor, religion, human relations!"

And so in *What Is Art?* Tolstoy sets out by ridiculing art's dependence as art upon taste, smell, touch, hearing as mere specializations of "taste" (in the sense of personal preference) and catering only to sensual pleasure. For it is in the interest of pleasure that there occurs a "shifting [of] the question of beauty to the question of taste," especially because it was influenced by Enlightenment thinkers such as Voltaire and Diderot. European thought has corrupted Russian understanding of the use proper to art, so that the flood of aesthetic argument in the nineteenth century "is not only not useful, but is even harmful." As for the relation of our sensual experiences in service to art, Tolstoy's "sight'" as paramount is defensible, but perhaps not so on the hidden grounds to his argument at last. One need only examine the marvels of texture in *War and Peace* or *Anna Karenina* – that great novel in which is most central one creature who becomes infatuated with another – or that later triumph *The Death of Ivan Ilych* (1886). In doing so, we discover in Tolstoy a gift of "negative capability" through sensual imagery in a greatness of his own art. It is an accomplishment which haunts him increasingly.

In the opening chapter of *What Is Art?* he gives us a sensually palpable account of his experience of a rehearsal of a very poor opera. There he engages imagery summoning all our senses to a response, to a rejection of pseudo-artists as discredited through Tolstoy's command of and deployment of complex imagery. That same talent – gift – summons sympathetic response to his Ivan in an excruciating pathos as he here uses to castigate false artists born of false aesthetics, in his view. By his command of images, vested by our own sensual experiences, we are likely to join with Tolstoy in rejecting artists as social parasites. But what we discover subsequently is that what is most disturbing to Tolstoy is not that these pseudo-artists exist as parasites of society. It is rather their serving a tendency to elevate art as supreme, as does Schiller. Tolstoy will become increasingly uneasy about his own work, tending to see it as an effect of a sinfulness in him, since art by its nature is dependent upon the sensual world. There is an irony, then, in the effectiveness of the art he uses in attacking the performance of that opera he attends. And we have a sense of having been present vicariously through his skillfulness with images and therefore moved to consent to the authority of his judgment because he so vividly stirs our participation in his remembrance. But here our terms *vividly* and *sense* are larger to our several senses themselves in rousing our response than merely a "sight" imagery. Why, then, Tolstoy's concern lest the other senses intrude upon art's domain? They intrude, he objects, to such a degree that there are now published treatises on the "art of the sense of taste . . . of smell . . . of touch . . . of hearing" as well as "of sight."

What is increasingly discomforting to Tolstoy, after *War and Peace*, is the problem of the senses in relation to spiritual ends, so that the body becomes progressively a diabolic burden of the soul for him. He moves toward Manichaeanism. The irony that haunts him is that his special gifts are those of the artist. But art cannot avoid the senses, for it cannot avoid nature as known through the senses. We may see that his elevation of sight in respect to the question of beauty, then, is an elevation of that one of our several senses that is most suitable to our keeping a distance from created reality, though we cannot sever absolutely our engagement by creation even through our sight. To blind oneself, alas, may serve only to exacerbate the burden upon consciousness of the remaining senses. Traditionally, the eye is taken as the gateway of the soul, understood traditionally as opening the soul to the world. If we "gaze deeply into" another's eyes, we may glimpse something of his essential nature as soul. But if one would withstand such intrusion, one's best defense is that avenue of intrusion, the gate to the soul more effectively defended than other gates of the senses – though sight-imagery may in the end prove to be a Trojan horse.[1] On the other hand, what protection has one from decibels? Or from rancorous odors, or the taste of poorly prepared food? Indeed, from the feel of intrusive objects upon the touch – a limb falling on one's head or the palpable experience of a car crash?

Even for the sight, there are possible traumatic intrusions, as the bloodily graphic body counting on the evening television news shows. Or in a different dimension, there may be an encounter with a "blinding" light, or darkness may seal physical vision. Those natural possibilities to the faculty of sight, indeed, have served metaphor from the time of the Greeks, from the time of the Gospels. It serves metaphorically as well in that traumatic experience Tolstoy writes of to his wife, occurring at a small place called Arzamas in the late summer of 1869. In deep night before flickering candles, he engages this sense of sight in relation to spiritual terror. A sense of anxiety overwhelms him, wakes him, with no apparent cause. (He is happily married, a celebrated poet with *War and Peace* in its final installment.) He awakens in that state about two in the morning, and his guttering candles serve him not at all with any relief. He orders the horses harnessed and sets out for home before dawn, fleeing he knows not what.

Commenting on the experience as recalled by Tolstoy, Lev Shestov suggests that "An abyss had opened before him which threatened to swallow him." What he saw was "the triumph of death on earth, he saw himself a living corpse." Perhaps he saw something very like what Eliot in his own moment of crisis saw, reflected in the irony of Eliot's

---

1   One of the thematic evidences to those dealing with psychopaths is that in looking into such a creature's eyes they prove unyielding but bottomless. See Robert D. Hare's *Without Conscience: The Disturbing World of the Psychopaths Among Us.*

"Whispers of Immortality" as beginning with Webster, who was "much possessed by death / And saw the skull beneath the skin; / And breathless creatures under ground / Leaned backward with a lipless grin." Tolstoy will revisit that terror henceforth. Richard Pevear in his "Preface" to *What Is Art?* very aptly summons Konstantin Levin from Tolstoy's next major novel, *Anna Karenina* (1877). Levin reflects that "In infinite time, in the infinity of matter, in infinite space, a bubble-organism separates itself, this bubble holds out for a while and then bursts, and this bubble is me." That is the terror for Tolstoy, leading him at last to a rejection of creation itself, in which alone is there possible time or matter or space impinging upon the isolated bubble of the self which ceases to exist at death. Levin looks about him, with the same sense of the walking dead that Eliot attributes to Webster. The young, the old, the working peasants he commands – all are doomed. For they, as Levin says, even as the "heavy-bellied horse, breathing rapidly with flared nostrils" as it turns the grinding wheel are doomed. "And moreover, not only they, but I, too, will be buried and nothing will be left. What for?" If Tolstoy somewhat rescues Levin from despair in the final pages of the novel, he is not himself rescued. For always, wherever the senses lead him, those senses reveal only death, oblivion, lying beneath the skin of whatever the senses engage.

It will lead Tolstoy to that "philosophy" that made him world-famous, in which he preaches a Church of Christ without Christ – to recall a companion philosopher to Tolstoy, though a fictional one who appears upon the intellectual scene much later. That is Hazel Motes's studied attempt against that terror, dramatized by Flannery O'Connor in *Wise Blood*. Hazel is a driven man, a Christ-haunted man, even as is Tolstoy in his actual life. One can only reflect on the dark circumstances of each at his end. Hazel is self-blinded in his boarding room, his body wrapped with barbwire. Tolstoy, fleeing a world proximately represented by his ceaselessly devoted wife, herself a steady Orthodox Christian, comes to die in a remote railway town, surrounded by government troops, his family in a civil war over possessing him in his last moments. And, of course, there is the horde of media vultures making Tolstoy's death the spectacular "media event" to the world as we still remember it.

If his wife Sonya was a devout Orthodox Christian, Tolstoy had long since rejected the Church – all its sacraments and mystery. The sacraments and the mystery of the Incarnation make an intimate relation of "form and matter," in a rescue as seen by the Orthodox of creation itself. Tolstoy rejects that rescue with Voltaire's scorn. No one since Voltaire has been so scathing of those mysteries central to the Orthodox Christian, East or West: the Scandal of Particularity, the Advent of God himself in a rescue of creation – the historical intersection of the transcendent and immanent in a supreme sacrifice. But Voltaire is so moved, not by Tolstoy's terror but by the intellectual intention of power over creation through knowledge, in an embrace of time, space, matter. Tolstoy's scornful rejection is of both the transcendent and of the immanent, in an elevation of himself as the singular spiritual reality. If in doing so he appears to himself a savior of humanity as generalized in the concept of suffering, he appears quite other to Maxim Gorky. Gorky, a revolutionary in political exile, visits Tolstoy at the time Tolstoy is in religious exile, excommunicated by the Orthodox Church. Gorky recalls the experience of attempted conversation. "Suddenly the old Russian lord, the arrogant aristocrat would spring up behind the stage costume of *muzhik* beard and rumpled blouse, and then the friends and partners in conversation would feel a chill down their spines and turn pale." If Chekhov is less angry than Gorky, he is baffled by Tolstoy as peasant-in-residence at the estate at Yasnaya Polyana. Gorky, on the other hand, an intimate of Tolstoy's in their Eastern exile, attempting conversation on high political and social matters, finds Tolstoy confusing himself with God and deporting himself in argument with the "authoritarianism of a provincial governor."

Tolstoy is beloved to a larger world more distant from him than Sonya's proximity as keeper of his image, or than Gorky as recruiter to social and political causes close at hand, and that larger world celebrates him as if he were a savior. Tolstoy strengthens the sentimentality possible by that distance by declaring as the only admissible icon suited to the ideal of humanity the peasant, an argument making converts, many of them to be subsequently converted to Marxist "humanitarianism." The peasant is holy because he has no education, is illiterate. He owns no portion of the world. And that doctrine, alas, will be appropriated presently by Lenin. At Tolstoy's death, Lenin writes several pieces in praise of the old man – in preparation for that political movement which will erase all hierarchy in nature, but most especially in social and political nature. In that triumph, the state will itself cease to exist, the argument goes. Such is Lenin's promise. Meanwhile, Tolstoy has exercised a considerable influence toward the abolition of the Church – in contrast to Dostoyevsky, who struggles for its recovery. If the Church is seemingly wounded mortally in the name of humanity – in Tolstoy's view – his other enemy, the State, already seems not long for this world.

In desperate flight, then, Tolstoy still has a glimmer of light – a hint of doubt as to his righteousness as Manichaean. At his death, he is reading with some suggestion of desperateness – or rather rereading – Dostoyevsky's *Brothers Karamazov*. He might well have reread *Crime and Punishment*, a novel published in alternate portions alongside *War and Peace*. Had he done so, he might have recognized how deeply affected he was all along by Cartesian Idealism and Kantian transcendentalism, positions he attempted to exorcise from his mind. These had also influenced the rise of political Nihilism in Tolstoy's and Dostoyevsky's intellectual circles.

Tolstoy attempted to put aside those early influences, scathing in his rejections of all Western philosophy – by which he means principally post-Cartesian philosophy. But his early fascination with Western thought had struck too deeply into his intellect. So deep as to lie buried under his own attempts to make himself an indestructible bubble. His "thought" led him to the conclusion that in defense against the appetites of the body, castration might even be necessary. He attempted to divest himself of all worldly things, dressing in peasant garb and demanding of his wife peasant fare. But he continued to be potent sexually and continued to be a resident on his considerable estate, which Sonya struggled to maintain – Tolstoy having given away all property and copyrights. Death was an ultimate escape dictated by his principles, involving him fancifully with the idea of suicide. But he died "naturally," an old man in a final terror at that wayside railroad station Astapovo, grieved by the popular press and by sentimental intellectuals around the world.

ii

Descartes, in his *Discourse on the Method*, observes in a tone of lament: "[S]ince we have all been children before being men, and since it has for long fallen to us to be governed by our appetites and our teachers . . . it is almost impossible that our judgments should be so excellent or solid as they should have been had we had complete use of our reason since our birth, and had we been guided by its means alone." Tolstoy takes the converse, regretting not having been also born grown but without any corrupting influence of *reason*, and so therefore devoted to pure feeling. "Feelings," he says, "the most diverse, very strong and very weak, very significant and very worthless, very bad and very good, if only they infect the reader, the spectator, the listener, constitute the subject of art." *Feeling* brought to signs and *infecting* another: that is art.

Descartes' hero, then, becomes the mathematician as pure scientist, purified through reason deployed to abstractionism. Tolstoy's hero is the peasant, not only because the peasant (unlike Tolstoy) is especially blessed by possessing no worldly property, but is more fully blessed in contrast to Tolstoy by never having become literate and highly educated. Meanwhile, the educated artist Tolstoy must make the most of his curse. Thus art most simply taken may somewhat alleviate the burden of property and the curse of reason he has derived from reading. Art, rationalized in the name of feeling, may displace reason imposed by a false science at the expense of feeling. Tolstoy rises to rhetorical passion in that long labor *What Is Art?* in which he advocates spontaneous feeling over studied thought. Feeling is to be made a means to any possible rescue of man from the evil of having been born into the flesh – though as well involving a submission to suffering the flesh. One might slyly suggest as much, especially if one is so irreverent a presence to Tolstoy as Maxim Gorky. Against such sly irony, Tolstoy is adamant. Art's end is a communion of hapless individuals through feeling purged of thought.

His argument nevertheless leads him to an entrapment, for he can only argue by the means of reason against reason itself. That necessity kindles a passion bordering on anger in him. *"Art is that human activity which consists in one man's consciously conveying to others, by certain external signs, the feelings he has experienced, and in others being infected by those feelings and also experiencing them."* These words he sets in italics, a shout against reason's presumptions in decreeing the nature of art, which he has himself already demanded be defined abstractly, independent of any manifestation of a thing as art. Thus his most severe objection to the proliferating industry of aesthetic criticism in his day:

> Instead of giving a definition of true art and then, depending on whether a work fits or does not fit this definition, judging what is and what is not art, a certain series of works found pleasing for some reason by people of a certain circle is recognized as art, and a definition such as will include all these works is then invented.

And so Tolstoy would establish his own counter circle, nevertheless defining art abstractly out of the hidden grounds of a terror born out of the presence to him of existential reality, the skin hiding death and oblivion. By his counter-abstractionism, which he implies to be free of the distortions of merely "inventing" a definition, he would measure works of art independent of their actualities as they exist as whatever thing each work is. Hiding the actual grounding of his intended abstract definition – his terror of the actual world impinging upon his sensual nature (the inescapable dimension of reality to art) – he takes refuge in a concept inescapably associated with that very dimension of human nature as *incarnate* being: *feeling*, not *reason*, is the essence of art. His hero stands, largely speechless, before him at every turn: the long-suffering peasant, an icon suited to Tolstoy's vision of himself as suffering the burden of existing in the body.

The peasant becomes his icon, a holy presence to be approached through feeling and emulated by feeling in opposition to intrusive thought and all of thought's physical and metaphysical questions. But in this approach to human kind through pure feeling (as opposed to Kantian pure thought), in the event the roused sympathy for human suffering creates a community of sentimental intelligentsia scattered around the world, intellectual converts to a vague feeling called *humanitarianism*. It is a dislocation of intellect which will prove convenient in the decade after Tolstoy's death, to Lenin and his followers as we observed. Out of Tolstoy's own abstract definitions of art as justified by feeling at the expense of reason, in the name of the peasants of the world, Lenin will relocate that vague spiritual concern which serves so well to reduce intellect to sentimentality, turning that sentimentality to a devotion to the science of Marxist economics as salvational. Thus Tolstoy inadvertently contributes to Lenin's reconstruction of reality, the reality that so terrified Tolstoy – the reality of nature and human nature. Lenin will decree and enforce what is implicit in Tolstoy and the source of his terror: a materialistic limit to man's nature.

As for such abstract definitions of art as Tolstoy's and then Lenin's, Aristotle was and is sounder. Aristotle would seek definition in relation to the realities of the things to be defined – *cow* or *poem*. Thus he looks at lyrics, at plays, at histories, and seeks by reason to discover what they reveal as common. Tolstoy presumes himself already possessed of a definition of "true art" independent of actual works of art because it is derived from his moral outrage against reality. He would then exercise a pragmatic Manicheanism whose arbiter is himself. He needs only replacing by Lenin, and the pragmatic Manicheanism shifted to materialism from Tolstoy's abstract idealism, to summon most of those Tolstoyeans converted by the old man. There occurs a new conversion to the cause of materialistic Marxism. What wonder, then, that the liberal humanitarianism (against which Dostoyevsky sets himself) commits itself to materialistic Marxism?

And so the champion of *reason*, for whom thought is the highest end for man, Descartes, is answered by the champion of *feeling* as man's highest state, Tolstoy. Tolstoy is nevertheless a child of Descartes, reacting by rejecting that father to his thought 250 years after Descartes. He does so in an insufficiently radical opposition. In the interval of years between them (Descartes to Tolstoy) one sees occurring in Western and Eastern (Russian) intellect evidence of the erosion of intellect by self-centering Idealism. T. S. Eliot speaks of it in our century as the "dissociation of sensibilities," the "separation of thought and feeling," which Eliot first discovers as the erosive weakness in that poetry commonly called "Romantic." The Romantic makes feeling ultimate. But in that interval from Descartes to Tolstoy, however, the dissociation occurs in not only poetry but science and philosophy and theology as well, disciplines of intellect effecting consenting victims to that separation. It is the interval in recent intellectual history within which we discover the rise of that Modernist intellect whose fundamental principle becomes more rigidly insistent that the specific intellect is autonomous, its sovereignty self-decreed. Thus the individual intellect would set itself against any transconscious reality, a rejection deemed sufficient unto itself.

In *What Is Art?* Tolstoy would set himself against the varieties of aestheticians born of this dissociation, suddenly flooding both East and West with books in pursuit of "beauty" as "pleasure." The salons of Moscow, Petersburg, Paris, London are agog with highly sophisticated and (for Tolstoy) pseudo-philosophical arguments addressing the literati and would-be literati. In his recognition of the superficiality of these highly sophisticated arguments, justifying art to an age increasingly besieged by the powers of science on the one hand and by the social and political unrest on the other, Tolstoy becomes increasingly outraged. His criticism is of the esoteric defense of beauty as an abstract ideal existing in a Kantian transnatural universality on the one hand, and on the other hand an art as a sensual fillip suited to materialistic lusts. Following his detailed survey of numerous arguments – Italian, German, French, English, Russian, American – justifying aesthetics to these ends, he concludes that, "We call beauty in the subjective sense that which affords us a certain kind of pleasure. In the objective sense, we call beauty something absolutely perfect which exists outside us." But the Russian is less pretentious as we have seen. "In Russian, by the word *krasota* ['beauty'] we mean only that which is pleasing to the sight." He is rather insistent that "we can say 'beautiful' only of what is pleasing to our sight. So that the word and concept 'good' includes within itself the concept 'beautiful,' but not vice versa: the concept 'beautiful' does not cover the concept 'good.'"

If Tolstoy is largely right in rejecting the confusions of the multiple aesthetic theories at the close of the 19th century, he fails in not first establishing clearly a relation of beauty to the good. That is, he does not establish for his position the grounds of a defense oriented by an understanding of human nature itself, only reacting to the terms as defined by those whom he opposes. He does so in large part because, as fiercely as he seems to defend art, he always feels art itself but a final evidence of existential reality as itself corrupt and corrupting. Existence save as pure spirit is evil. From the time of

Anna Karenina, his sense of guilt for being an artist grows, art being to Tolstoy a curse such as Dostoyevsky felt his gambling to be. Beauty? Pleasure? Happiness? What have these to do with absolute (abstract) purity? They can only be evidence of corruptible man's responses to the material world, of man's sinfulness in his pursuit of sensual "pleasures" as an end. It is a burden made inescapable to him because of his body. As he told Gorky, revealing that burden: "Man can endure earthquake, epidemic, dreadful disease, every form of spiritual torment; but the most dreadful tragedy that can befall him is and will remain the tragedy of the bedroom." What he cannot accomplish, then, is a rescue of realities underlying those concepts derived from our experiences of reality: *pleasure, reason, beauty, happiness*. Both the terms and the reality giving rise to them are being corrupted by Modernism, as Tolstoy realizes. But he cannot adequately address the cause of that corruption. And so he is vaguely drawn by a desire for spirit purified of all matter, turning fanatic in his pursuit of that desire. He sees increasingly creation itself as diabolic, associating it with his own body. The happiness he seeks is through a distortion of his own given nature, a distortion which proves (from the perspective of Thomistic Realism) a desire for a vague species of nonexistence. He is, in this respect, drawn to death as if it were life – drawn to the void which he struggles to make substantial through his signs. But signs, first and last, bind intellect willy-nilly to the reality of creation. And so it proves Tolstoy's reason, dislocated.

iii

Let us address Tolstoy's dilemma from a radical position, one differing from that of Modernism and its concentration on material existence as confining man to a closed world on the one hand and from that of Tolstoy's reaction toward neo-Manichaeanism. Both are, from this radical address, species of intellectual error, bearing unsuspected kinship as error. *Beauty* is perceived by intellect in things. *Happiness* seems desired by intellect as if the end of desire's hope for fulfillment. But lacking an understanding of the relation of beauty to the desire for happiness, beauty itself may prove confounding to desire. That is, intellect may become confounded in misunderstandings of the nature of that concept *beauty,* which St. Augustine says is the language through which created things speak to the discrete soul.

Not recognizing the signified content of that language as necessary to understanding, intellect may become careless or impatient in its quest for a fulfillment of desire on its journey from birth to death here within this arena in which beauty is first encountered. To do so, especially under the dictates of Modernism's reduction of the arena of beauty to material existence suited only to temporal appetite, leaves intellect mired in the local, to the proximate as if that were the primary end of its own nature. For in that error, a fulfillment of appetitive nature seems primary to desire. Especially, we become centered in materialism as determinate of limits to intellect itself. If we react against this now pervasive doctrine we are calling Modernism as Tolstoy attempts to do – through a Manichaean rejection of material existence perceived through created things – we may (as Tolstoy seems to have done) end in an empty spiritualism.

Thus proximate ends, by a reductionism favoring dislocated desire, pursues the proximate and secondary as if ultimate. What is lost is the possibility of a perfection of the limited gifts to the intellectual soul incarnate, the person, through a recovery of an orientation to his proper end. That is a tendency toward the possibility of a limited perfection as person insofar as person is free of confusing temptation to secondary ends as if ultimate. That possible (but limited) perfection is through temporal ends engaged by proportionate stewardship to those temporal ends. Tolstoy certainly is moved by a charity toward creation as many of his gestures show, though he elects the illiterate peasant out of all creation as alone worthy of his charity. Thus on an occasion he serves on a soup line.

What is lost on either hand is any prospect of understanding the simple unity of person implied in the naming of the person as an *intellectual soul incarnate*. Tolstoy feels driven to reject the properties of the *intellectual* and the *incarnate* to his given nature as person, out of his desire for pure spirit. It is that pure spirit, purged of material dimensions, that becomes the ultimate Beauty for Tolstoy. Were he in this pursuit recovered by reason to the implications of that desire (whereby he must come to an accommodation of the beauty of created things), he would avoid that Manichaean denigration of creation, seeing its limited beauty in relation to that Perfect Beauty intuitively desired as a fulfillment of his person. We speak of this as Beatitude. That failing, his concern focuses upon the desired beauty of his own soul purged of both intellect and body, an exclusion of his own complex nature as person, as intellectual soul incarnate. In this dislocation of desire what is the most probable effect is an ideological intensity turning toward self-worship. That, perhaps, is the inclination in Tolstoy of which Gorky is so scornful.

As for the alternate excess, the tendency toward beauty believed restricted to material dimensions, what is compromised is our desire to contemplate and revere beauty in the light of a recognition of its transcendent Cause. Thus the distortion of innate desire for the beautiful concentrates the intellectual self upon a fulfillment of a partial appetitive nature to the self. And so when the person pursues beauty as if an object to be possessed, which possession he supposes effects a happiness of his self, the disposition to possessiveness of beautiful things can and often does effect an ugliness in the soul itself. The error lies in the supposition that by possession of a lesser good absolutely, that good is made the greater. Thus the appetitive, determined by the will to be primary to the happiness of the soul, may especially reduce the person toward limits we speak of as animalistic. Happiness thus will

be taken to lie in a perfection of the person as but a biochem-
ical thing, the happiness increasingly made territorial
through excessive possessiveness.

We know all too well from our own experiences as persons, or from observing other persons, that in respect to our
desire for fulfillment through the appetitive property to our
nature as if it were the whole of our personhood, the actual
effect is not happiness but unhappiness. What we presume as
occurring is a turning outward. But that proves a turning only
in a limited sense. It is rather a perverse version of that opening outward to things which we call charity of spirit, the
action of love. For the action of love is to be made in a sacrificial mode, an affectionate recognition of the beautiful thing as
beautiful because it is the very thing it is. Only in the limited
sacrifice of stewardship to that thing is some aspect of possession present. When St. Thomas defines beauty as that
which when seen pleases, he is speaking of this response to
the created nature of a beautiful thing. And, we must add, the
thing insofar as it is perfected according to its own given – its
created – nature, it is to be recognized as beautiful, its actual
beauty independent of mere taste. That is the aspect of beauty Tolstoy overlooks in declaring modern aesthetics devoted
only to diverse tastes. He is correct in his criticism of certain
distortions, but his attempted rescue from that distortion
lacks a sufficient metaphysical grounding for him to rescue
beauty by his understanding of it in the world.

In St. Thomas's definition of beauty, then, he is concerned
that we recover an ordinate response to the created nature of
beautiful things, a response quite distinct from that action of
possessiveness. St. Augustine had come to this recognition, in
his *Confessions,* in remembering his own intellectual action
toward created things. Turning from possessiveness he begs a
response from those things perceived by his senses. Having
heard a tentative response ("We are not God whom you
seek"), he demands from them, from "all those things that
stand around the doors of my flesh": "Tell me of my God!
Although you are not he, tell me something of him!" And

they answer with a "a mighty voice." Their "answer was their beauty." Thus speaks the philosophical saint. Our poets, from the time of the *Iliad* and *Odyssey*, have pursued dramatically this mystery of beauty as at once within the world and beyond the world. As for us at the lag-end of our millennium, if not Helen of Troy as a beautiful thing complicating our journey as *homo viator*, occasioning the play of person in high drama since Homer, or if not a Beatrice to Dante, we yet encounter this same tensional concern for the intellectual soul incarnate for the mystery of the beautiful. Think only of the multitude of popular dramas in which the Hope Diamond replaces Helen or Beatrice as magnet to a dramatic tensional conflict, a tension between a celebration of beauty and a possession of beauty – though of course some Helen and more rarely some Beatrice may also be present as a complication.

Now a pursuit of beauty as if it were to be merely possessed tends to mire careless or impatient intellect in appetitive materialism (and Tolstoy's objection to art's end as "beauty" castigates it as "lust"). As often as not intellect's pursuit of local happiness as desire's proper end leads it to the isolation in some species of idealism reduced to ideology. Between these two false poles, Tolstoy is held in a frustrated tension of anger against existence itself. Such danger becomes an unhappiness leading the person to a rejection of actual material creation itself, as Tolstoy tends to do. Put another way, intellect pursuing effects as ends proves inevitably Manichaean, whether it rejects the material aspects of person on the one hand (as does the idealist) or the spiritual aspects of person on the other (as does the materialist). Both would make an *effect* the initiating *cause* of *desire*.

In our own radical perspective upon reality (the Thomistic perspective), the proper cause to a pursuit of happiness is the same on either hand: namely, the *truth of things as experienced*. And so that is why St. Thomas says in praise of art, concerning *homo viator* as journeyman intellect charged to an accommodation to secondary effects, and here specifically in respect to *beauty* as the language between intellect and beautiful things, that "beauty is that which when seen pleases." Tolstoy to the contrary ridicules *pleasure* as related to beauty. But he must do so by a reductionism whereby pleasure is assigned as possible only to the appetitive. We can only conclude that the advocacy of pleasure in art has as its end "lust," a conclusion which leaves him unhappy with the beauty of his own made things. Similarly, he ridicules what he calls "metaphysical" aesthetics, which posits beauty as a thing in itself, transcendent and separate and counter to the appetitive reduction to pleasure. But Tolstoy does so only because his principle enemy – the Kantian philosophy of his youth – is the limit he allows to "metaphysical" questions. He does not engage, except superficially, the relation of the truth of things to the Cause of things in order to find an ordinate vision, a prospect upon man's proper ends. His own personal species of Manichean idealism becomes ultimately devoted not to God but to the void, though he calls it God. And in emptying himself of his own created nature insofar as he can, he recreates his own spirit in that image. Tolstoy at last would reject all things, the very rejection seeming to him his only rescue from the "sin" of his attraction to things existing as perceived through his body. This Puritan of Nothingness maintains his argument in response to an overwhelming sense of his own sinfulness, making his primary devil *sex* but *material possession* a kindred devil. Significantly, Tolstoy very studiously sets up the West as the source of this contamination of his soul. But in doing so, he limits his range of reflection to the post-Renaissance – from Descartes to Kant to Schopenhauer. From our perspective on his intellectual actions, he appears more deeply affected by these rationalists than his own reason reveals to him.

Out of such speculative concern for Tolstoy's ideology of the self, St. Thomas emerges more and more a sane intellectual presence, given the chaos of intellect as divided against itself in the Renaissance and Post-Renaissance world in both the East and West. He would no doubt remind us that beauty is not a metaphysical reality as a thing. It is an effect of one's truly seeing created things in their essential natures. It is in this perspective that one may discover that Providence, the creating and sustaining cause of things in their actualities and potentialities, affords us by that act a *pleasure* attendant upon our first seeing and then understanding a thing in itself. By that seeing and understanding, we know as concomitant both beauty and happiness as speaking to intellect the truth of the thing we experience. But these are secondary to the enlargement of our personhood through such experience. And by understanding we come to know as well that the thing truly seen cannot itself become ultimate end, for that is to succumb to the deportment of idolatry. Rather, what the truth of the thing says through the language of beauty is in anticipation of the proper end of *homo viator*. What it says is that both person and thing are created – *depend from* that Cause which is the ultimate end for *homo viator* as the Perfect Beauty. This was the recognition which turned St. Augustine from his own vacillating Manichaeanism – from his indulgences of the appetitive which then in his revulsion tempted him to a rejection of the things of creation. He turns from lust to a denial of a proper love of things as possible, and he does so in the name of an abstract and empty love called idealism, which he will subsequently attribute to Plato. But then at a crucial moment of his journey comes that moment we have cited when he commands "all the things that stand around the doors of [his] flesh" to speak truth. They do so, and in speaking this truth they also speak the truth he seeks. Theirs proves a "mighty voice" that dissolves St. Augustine's dilemma, so that he can at last come to terms with the *simplicity* of his own essential nature. For as person he is (1) intellectual (2) soul (3) incarnate – a simple nature. In him – by that nature – inhere the accidents of simplicity: he is appetitive creature as well as spiritual. And so if made appetitive in part, were he to deny the sensual as good, he would implicitly deny the Creator of that good.

When we lose this vision, by losing unified sensibilities proper to our unified nature, we will in the end create hopeless ways to a recovery. Consider the popular slogan that in America at least is taken as high certification of the sovereignty of person in relation to the state. We have a right to *life, liberty*, but most especially to the pursuit of *happiness*. It is a sequence which posits happiness as an ultimate end. How could we not come, at the close of our century, to the chaos of sovereignties – each person an autonomous state pursuing an effect (happiness) as if it were the ultimate end to our fundamental, essential nature.

St. Thomas would surely remind us, as Dante reminds us in his great *Comedy*, that when we pursue the Good through the good of things, the Cause of actual created things as ultimate end, the *pleasure* of both beauty and a happiness may prove attendant. Those effects may follow our consent to the truth of things, our consent to creation as good. Beauty and happiness as attendant effects of our experiences of reality in its multitudinous finite truths as things in themselves: these are graces added to right-mindedness and right-heartedness of intellect itself. Intellect, unified in sensibilities, approaches its own limited perfection through its proportionate consent as intellect to the truth of things as those things exist essentially, in their own discrete natures, in the recognition of which we hear them cry out, "He made us!" There follows upon hearing that cry in some degree of grace an experience of effects we would call beauty and happiness. It is through our sensible proportionate love as present in communion with things that we may be raised toward a vision of that Absolute Love. The anticipation of Beatitude – not a demand for instant possession of happiness and beauty unflickering in worldly experiences of creation. Rather, the anticipation stirred in us by effects of that openness is called love. It is an openness which only *falsely* can isolate the sensual and the spiritual, in a reduction destructive of that mysterious unity of a most wondrous thing: our self as a person, an intellectual soul incarnate. The sensual properties of our simple nature as person, St. Thomas says, initiates our first movement toward the Cause of creation.

iv

Our argument has been counter to both Modernist confusions which Tolstoy himself opposes, and to the even more confused "spiritual" dimension of Tolstoy's position in which he reveals conglomerate elements of a denatured Christianity and his own Modernist gnosticism, to which he seems oblivious, generating in his argument a cloudy reaction to existential reality. We return now to evidences of these confusions in order to reveal something of his influence as one of the fathers of current spiritual and moral bankruptcies of our intellectual community, largely dominant as we draw to the close of our own century. For although Tolstoy did not *intend* to do so, we may say out of charity, he rather certainly is still one of the contributing fathers to our chaos a hundred years (almost exactly) after he published his passionate outcry, *What Is Art?* We, too, argue from a concern for art's possible service to our rescue from confused wondering about the human condition. But we see such rescue possible only through reasoned recognitions of and understandings of our actual experiences of reality as the measure of the concepts long held as common in our talk about the human condition – so long common indeed as to have lost ground in the realities of experience and become abstractions, though they still stir in us "feelings" when uttered.

In Chapter XIII of his little book, Tolstoy recalls his forced attendance, out of social courtesy, of Wagner's *Nibelungen*, giving us that painful minute-by-minute account of that Nietzschean extravaganza. It is an art of the "big city mob," a "senseless, crude, false work, which has nothing to do with art," he says. Its effect ought to be "achieved in a still quicker way by drinking wine or smoking opium." It is this last twist which sharpens a recognition of a considerable weakness in Tolstoy, quite separate from any concern for the justness of his evaluation of the work itself. That is, as his account reveals, Tolstoy lacks a sense of humor. He has wit, but he is even uncomfortable with that rhetorical gift, most probably because wit cannot at last be dissociated entirely from thought, from reason, from common sense as common sense may be raised by rhetorical art to satiric ends. One need not be highly educated, of course, to be possessed of a wit that may be developed through native reason. But deep down Tolstoy always suspects that his special advantage as a member of the landed gentry and his education account for that wit. It is not native to human nature. And so he seems ashamed of evidencing wit with any direct intention to a rhetorical strategy as if it necessarily destroys a high seriousness. Not that he doesn't sometimes forget himself, but when he does so, it is most usually through an angry passion, so that his wit becomes fiercely sarcastic. Hence, when he attacks the Orthodox Church, except for the anger, he sounds Voltairean.

As for the absence of humor in him, he gives us what becomes at last, by its fullness, a tedious account of his boredom when trapped by friends into attending Wagner's opera. In summarizing the second act, after some attention to details rendered with exasperated sarcasm, he concludes: "This is all so stupid, so farcical, that one wonders how people older than seven can seriously attend it; yet thousands of quasi-educated people sit there, listening and watching attentively admiring it." He at last "rushed from the theatre with a feeling of revulsion that I still cannot forget." Whether the revulsion is from false art is a more complex question given the context he allows us, for he immediately concerns himself with what his ideal person would make of such a performance, a person that is, "respectable, intelligent, literate village labourer – one of those intelligent, truly religious men whom I know among the people." (The text here seems corrupt, since it is doubtful that Tolstoy would praise his labourer as "literate" rather than "illiterate.")

What is most scandalous to him is that given such "art," "millions of working days are spent to produce objects. . . incomprehensible in painting, music, drama," to speak nothing of novels and poems. "If not millions, at least hundreds of thousands of copies" of such poems and stories "are typeset and printed." And for what? To satisfy the poet and perhaps a friend. For as this quasi-artist (poet, musician, painter) will say in defending himself from criticism, he practices his art for "a very small number of the elect. . . . a best friend, one's own self." Just how millions in circulation become thus reduced to one or two is accounted for by the pretentiousness of the "city mob," sold a bill of goods by the greed of the artist, by art criticism, and by art schools.

But why did Tolstoy himself, in his excruciating experience of the opera, not burst out laughing at the absurdities he describes? Certainly not from timidity or fear of public embarrassment. One is tempted, then, to see the reason to lie in his lacking a sense of humor. He is unable to laugh at absurdity except as a device of moral indignation serving anger. One might, indeed, take Tolstoy's details of his experience and imagine (without too much difficulty) what Mark Twain would have made of those absurdities. We have Twain in an analogous and extended send-up of Scott's romances in *Huck Finn* and in *A Connecticut Yankee at King Arthur's Court* as evidence. Or in a closer parallel to Tolstoy on Wagner, we have Twain's "Fenimore Cooper's Literary Offenses," which sets out by putting the "art critic" in his place, as Tolstoy would do with angry indignation and therefore less effectively accomplished than Twain's *tour de force* in pretending to be a high critic. Twain objects to the opinions of, "the Professor of English Literature at Yale, the Professor of English Literature at Columbia, and Wilkie Collins." They ought to let "persons talk who have read Cooper," namely Twain. Cooper's art "has some defects. In one place in *Deerslayer*, and in the restricted space of two-thirds of a page, Cooper has scored 114 offenses against literary art out of a possible 115." For instance, "Every time a Cooper person is in peril, and absolute silence is worth four dollars a minute, he is sure to step on a dry twig" and "alarm all the reds and whites for two hundred yards around."

Such is enough of Twain's irreverence for what he considers pseudo-art to make our point by comparison. And in making it we are reminded that Twain is celebrated as writing in a culmination of an American art which Tolstoy abhors. Twain does so out of what has been called "Frontier Humor." What we suggest is that it is a humor more fundamentally native to conditions of human endurance of life's vicissitudes than can be accounted for adequately in the term's *geography* and *history*. Tolstoy praises his peasants in similar circumstances, rejecting the high romance of Medieval kings and chieftains that continues as the matter of an art he finds most corrupt in the post-Renaissance world. It is an abhorrent "Romance" to Tolstoy which Twain makes use of in his *Connecticut Yankee at King Arthur's Court*. Tolstoy sees that nostalgic matter leading to the isolation of the poet, to the point at which the poet can only celebrate his own *ennui*. These are such writers as (for Tolstoy) Baudelaire and Verlaine and Mallarmé; in such dramatists as Ibsen; in such fiction writers as Kipling, all of whom he scornfully rejects. For those, alas, "the feelings of honour, patriotism and amorousness, which constitute the main content of present-day art, call up in a working man only perplexity, scorn or indignation."

The proper content of art, then, is that of the "life of the labouring man" which is infinitely diverse in "forms of labour and dangers connected with it on the sea or underground." Such is the opening of a Tolstoy sentence interminable, listing the rich diversity of peasant life toward the edge of infinity. The varieties of human experiences of laboring men as he sees them, however – with only a minor relief of the joy through suffering – are less joyful than trying, grim and unleavened by a relief of joy either in wit or humor. The Tolstoyean "high seriousness" of concern which evidences no comic relief in recognition of human participation in the impinging disorders of life must lack persuasiveness at last, as he himself should know from the works of art he has himself made on occasion, though his dominant commitment is to the darkness in earthly life. Contrast to the point William Faulkner's treatment of the Tolstoyean "labouring man" on Mississippi dry-scrabble land, in such a work as Faulkner's *The Hamlet* or in "Was" or "Spotted Horses." In those works we recognize a degree of "negative capability" in Faulkner that reveals his own knowing participation in the human condition, his recognition of a common willfulness beyond the dictates of nature as defined by history and geography as circumscribing the "life of the labouring man." And so more than accidents of geography or history appear evident as affecting the different perceptions of adversity in Faulkner and Tolstoy. Human nature itself, whether revealed in the peasant subjected to the lord and land in Russia or in Mississippi, involves the person as more complex than the stylized portrait tempting Tolstoy to abstractions of person whenever he turns to argument and away from his own gifts as poet.

Human nature, then, proves common to man though variously experienced in uncommon and accidental circumstances, diverse in the particularities of circumstance in the spectacle of nature and history. Such is that complex challenge to human endurance that art in its tribute may well require a humor beyond wit. Let us suggest, then, that humor is a virtue suited to understanding and wisdom, a necessity to our enduring the journey as *homo viator,* in recognition of the limits of the artist himself in his making no less than to *homo viator* in actualities. Wit, on the other hand, is amenable to intellectual knowing as a means to the imaginative uses of logic and as such modifies somewhat the participatory surrender to the common. They are not exclusive in our intellectual deportment, but they tend to differences in art's response to the mysteries of life as yet unriddled. Wit in its exercise affords a degree of self-protection from unriddled mystery, a distancing we often discover in the witty person whereby he may attain a detachment protecting him somewhat from participation in, or consent to, the common condition of his humanity as besieged within circumstantial existence. In literature, irony becomes the flavor of that detachment. Humor rises for us rather through an implicit recognition that by man's very nature as person, he cannot stand aside at last from the complexities of encroaching accidents upon his nature as a person. In that recognition, endurance is a virtue – a suffering of inescapable circumstances – which touches upon hope through humor. For by his very nature, man is born unto trouble as the sparks fly upward, as Job learned in his endurance, though neither wit nor humor proved salve to his suffering.

If Tolstoy thinks that the peasant's "struggle with nature, wild animals, his relations with domestic animals, his labors in the forest, the steppe, the fields, the orchard, the kitchen garden" is the stuff proper to art, the poet may nevertheless move beyond mere pathos dictated by that struggle, and by a humor beyond wit incarnate by his art our common fallen human nature. Faulkner's peasants prove humanly resonant at their horse trading games. One might even perhaps (though Tolstoy could only see absolute degeneracy in such an episode) summon that account in *The Hamlet* of the idiot Ike Snopes in his simple love of a cow, in which strange episode there seems mingled St. Francis's *agape* and an erotic animalism of man disoriented from love. (Ike Snopes, one suspects, is an idiot whom Dostoyevsky would recognize, judging from his concerns in *The Idiot*.) As Cleanth Brooks observes persuasively in his *Yoknapatawpha Country*, this seeming perversity as idyllically presented by Faulkner sets off "a deeper horror and a greater perversity, that of Flem Snopes . . . who has no poetry in him and no love at all." Faulkner, then, knows the peasant as person, even when depicting the peasant as reduced to primal nature as is Ike. And he knows through sharing an essential nature with even those landed gentry of Mississippi, those of Tolstoy's "city mob." In Faulkner there is a visionary penetration of human nature which Tolstoy comes to the edge of and then shies from in his deliberate address to the responsibility of art, so that in resolution he elevates his peasant to icon, weighing evil as summed by mere property and mere education. Faulkner's vision, then, requires humor in the face of horror itself, the most testing horror being that of the diminution of person. It requires more than disgust with circumstantial impingements in attempting to discover a proper meaning through art in celebration of the human condition, especially of course to respond to humanity submerged by false intellect, the particular trial to our attempt here to see Tolstoy with the charity required without neglecting the errors of his intellectual deportment.

Lacking a range and depth of vision into the human condition such as Faulkner's, or for that matter Dostoyevsky's own darker vision into the heart of darkness possible in man, Tolstoy is severely handicapped by comparison. For a Faulkner or a Dostoyevsky well knows those depths of human nature as present in both country peasants and Tolstoy's "city mobs" of the sophisticated intellectuals. And so his passionate *What Is Art?* proves to be a tract which by clever self-deception hoodwinks. But the principal victim of that hoodwinking at last is Tolstoy himself. He seems increasingly unable to accept his extraordinary gifts as poet because haunted increasingly by an overbearing guilt whose burden upon his conscience is difficult for him to identify. Certainly after *Anna Karenina* (1875–77) he is never more miserable than when he has written a very good story. Following that great novel, which he considered calling "Two Couples" or "Two Marriages," he begins a rapid intellectual decline into Manichaeanism, writing tract after tract in an attempt to exorcise that guilt.

One of the most curious of the lot of those numerous tracts undertaken from the 1870s to the end of his life is this engagement of a metaphysics of art as an anti-metaphysics. In a moralistic stance on behalf of simple unlettered and unpropertied humanity, he declares as true art that to which such peasants respond instinctively at once, rejecting by their response the flood of bad art. "There is," he says, "hardly one in a hundred thousand" works of the immeasurable flood of art things which can be called "true works of art." And at the last, he seems inclined to deny even that rarity. Indeed, his suspicion is that the peasant is endangered in proportion to his dependence upon art other than that immediate to him in the necessities of his labor – what we would ordinarily perhaps speak of as crafts. For writing and painting and composing music require a leisure inimical to those virtues possible only through labor for sheer survival. What one makes with his own hands appears to Tolstoy the highest reach of art, so that all his later life, when he is at times possessed as it seems to him by the demon muse seducing him to write stories, he struggles to reach the peasant's high but lowly art. One may imagine, then, his outrage should he be confronted by such argument as that of the Thomist Josef Pieper in *Leisure, The Basis of Culture.*

One of our own sentimental recollections of Tolstoy, usually treasured by those of us whom he would castigate as the comfortable and idle and educated rich, is of Tolstoy in peasant garb working at peasant tasks in a little room appointed like a monastic cell but within that large house he dominates but refuses to acknowledge as his family estate. Meanwhile, his wife Sonya and the children and the servants labor to provide amenable comfortable conditions to that withdrawn genius, who becomes at this stage of his life a vegetarian with a severity to his senses that makes abstinence from all but the simplest fare appear rather a species of gluttony defying the virtue of temperance. Chekhov protests having been "subjugated by the Tolstoyan philosophy . . . for some seventeen years." In fierce protest Chekhov declares that "reason and a sense of justice have convinced me that there is more love in electricity and steam than there is in chastity and the refusal to eat meat," at least as that deportment is tyrannically advocated by Tolstoy and his disciples. Chekhov and some others encounter Tolstoy at home and because of his genius are deferential to him in his peasant garb, busy at his cobbler's last. A Gorky, of course, reacts otherwise.

The highest reach of art (so Tolstoy tends to reflect in recovering from his fall into the sin of writing a story) is that which leads a man to "eat an egg laid by a hen he has raised, a bread grown in his own field, or an apple from a tree he has been tending for years." That way lies a progress wherethrough mankind develops a "religious consciousness" which "consists in recognizing the union of people as both the general and the individual aim of life," in which union lies no doubt admirable concepts of humanity gathered in a universal "uniting of mankind" into "a socialist state or commune," which people elsewhere might "recognize . . . as a world federation." Just how a man in such circumstances as were actually Tolstoy's could consider a hen his own hen or an apple tree his own tree or a field his own field is a problem not to be adequately addressed, though it will be addressed by Tolstoy's succeeding ideologist, Lenin, whose answer is that no one *owns* anything but each one *owns* everything. Meanwhile, before that development in political affairs, Tolstoy continues catered to by Sonya and the children and servants, including his illegitimate son who serves him as a coachman.

In his tract of definition, intending to make a true art legitimate to an audience incapable of recognizing that legitimacy – artists, art critics, art schools – Tolstoy grounds his position where, ironically, art soon will become pawn to the politically revolutionary arguments already underway, presented in the name of the masses by Lenin. At Tolstoy's death in 1910, Lenin writes those praiseful tributes to Tolstoy, hedging toward usurping art in the name of the people to the uses of political power. The irony lies in Lenin's philosophical inversion of Tolstoy's ground. Tolstoy argues for an abstract spiritual effect to be gained through *feelings* purged of *reason* and *logic*, whereby through "sincerity" (the artist's supreme virtue for Tolstoy) we meld into undifferentiated spiritual transcendence through that agency of feeling – into a universal soul. That is Tolstoy's version of Christianity – a Christianity specifically without Christ. Lenin, through the rigors of

Marxist materialism, administered by reductionist reason and ruthless logic, commands art to materialistic grounds as the social limit, that limit being the ultimate to human existence in Marxist ideology. Art therefore must be programmatic, a secondary servant to an ultimate materialistic society. For Tolstoy in his Manichaean spiritualism it is also secondary and difficult to distinguish at last from the Brahmanism of a willed self-salvation. For Lenin a materialistic restructuring of the given world to fit ideological structures enslaving the material world itself, especially man as biological creature, is the ultimate end. Both are positions undertaken in the name of humanity, of course, and both take origin in intellect's distortion of human nature as common, whereby we distinguish persons as specifically created intellectual souls incarnate.

V

If Tolstoy's "spiritual" Manichaeanism subordinates art to a Brahman-like universalism, the program as he intends it nevertheless engages the immediate social and political world within the grounds which Lenin will exploit. If we consider Tolstoy's "Conclusion" to *What Is Art?* we may see how amenable his argument proves to the revolution already underway in Russia as Tolstoy writes his treatise. This is a book, he says, which has occupied him for fifteen years. (It was first published in 1898, though finished earlier, and in an English translation approved by Tolstoy, since censorship delayed its Russian version.) What is of interest to our point – that Tolstoy's defense of art serves Lenin's cause – is evident in the conclusion by his turning from "true art" to the nature of "true science" and its relation to art. Along the way to conclusion, of course, he continues his fierce rejection of false art, often violent in his rhetoric out of moral indignation. He adds a spirit hardly spiritual to his concern, a spirit volatile enough to serve the shrewd manipulations of art just ahead who will emerge in the political and social chaos of the Marxist revolution.

Thus Tolstoy declares that "people who wish to live a good life should be directed towards destroying this [bad] art, because it is one of the cruelest evils oppressing mankind," more destructive even than the concentration of capital and land to the possession of an "upper-caste" who in their uses of art become for Tolstoy the "city mob." What we might see as most subversive of his own intent to the universal brotherhood of man is precisely the *directing* toward the good life to be accomplished by a "true science," which as *knowledge* is to be translated by "true art" into *feelings* sufficient to destroy any opposition through collective political power. It is a destruction akin to Nihilism, being "directed" in order to establish ideological good over reality. That Tolstoy, for all his reactionary arguments against totalitarian authority, is himself fundamentally totalitarian was recognized by Gorky, as we observed, who found him quite other than the champion of humanity that the world holds him to be. That broad and generous response by the larger world Gorky found baffling. As he wrote to Chekhov, "Leo Tolstoy does not love men . . . he judges them, cruelly and too severely." After all, Tolstoy had said to Gorky, coldly, "I am more a *muzhik* than you are and my feelings are more like a *muzhik's* than yours!" Gorky's is an insight into this "provincial governor" of morality that touches Tolstoy's depths.

In another letter, after his experiences with Tolstoy when both are in exile (Tolstoy excommunicated by the Church and Gorky by the state for his Marxist ideas), Gorky observes that Tolstoy "All his life . . . has hated death, all his life the 'horror of Arzamus' has been quivering inside him." And that hate had come increasingly to concentrate on the locus of death most immediate to him, his own body. But what Gorky sees as hatred of death is at last a hatred of life itself, as if life were an intimidation to be dominated by Tolstoy's version of the "soul" lest he become enslaved by weak uncertain life. "Why," asks Gorky in a letter to a friend, "Why should not nature make an exception to the rule, by giving him [Tolstoy], him alone, physical immortality, yes, why not?" Certainly

Tolstoy seems at points to cling to a feeling, through art argued the purifier of his consciousness, yielding a faith in a Manichaean immortality. Consciousness drains life of life, save when the angelistic consciousness is transformed by feeling and is thus enabled to keep death itself at bay. In his most considered argument toward that end, coming to his conclusion in *What Is Art?* he sees "true science" as ultimately justifying his instinct (as he would put it) for immortality, in which instinct life in the world is an action of death – a mystery unyielding to the terror of that haunting "horror of Arzamus."

And so in his "Conclusion" he pronounces "true science" to have as its proper end "arranging the lives of people," determining "how the overall life of mankind ought or ought not to be arranged, how to arrange sexual relations, how to bring up children, how to use land," and so on. Included as departments of "true science" are both "theology and philosophy," which provide "true" evidence upon which programs may be established to arrange the lives of people. The validity of theology and philosophy is measured by "the religious consciousness of the given time and society," which consciousness must not adhere at all to outworn philosophy and theology, for by such adherence a progress in perfecting "religious consciousness" is at risk. Thus false art is to be expunged – that of Dante and Shakespeare and Goethe and Beethoven and on and on, declared in a proscription by Tolstoy as self-anointed Pope of the new "spiritual consciousness." And to be discarded as well, all mythology and history inimical to the necessity of a forced perfection of the brotherhood of man. That rejection applies especially to all Church dogma, most especially to sacramental worship or to any pretenses to the divinity of Christ or to the redemption of man by Christ in the Incarnation. (These denials proved the grounds of Tolstoy's excommunication.)

All these doctrines are but sheer "superstition," propounded by a false church in order that it might suppress and control and exploit the proletariat. True "religious consciousness" is "the common religious consciousness of men . . . of the brother-hood of men and their well-being in mutual union." Indeed, that religious consciousness, to be established by "true science," "consists in recognizing the union of people as both the general and the individual aim of life," as we have heard him say. And that union becomes possible only when "true science" *prescribes the definitions* of that union, whereupon "true art" translates that true scientific evidence into feeling and "infects" the generality of mankind. Thus the formula of relationship: "True science studies and introduces into human consciousness the truths and knowledge which are regarded as most important by the people of a certain period and society. Art transfers these truths from the realm of knowledge to the realm of feeling." The synthesis is Hegelian, seen by Tolstoy as an infinite progression toward an end not of history but of a perfect universal "common religious consciousness of men." It is to be achieved through art by art's infection of individuals with feeling at each stage of this progress of "religious consciousness," out of which current stage the next step in that progress in the history of religious consciousness is to be made toward Tolstoy's Point Omega. True science of the latest established period and society, the present, must speak the truth of that new moment, whereupon art transfers that new truth into an infectious art, further melding humanity in a "union," toward the one and only acceptable manifestation in history of "true religion," "the uniting of all people into a socialist state or commune."

And this argument is from the artist whose feelings are more those of a *muzhik* than those of anyone he meets among scientists or artists, according to his haughty self-evaluations to Gorky. It is argument from an artist who is violently opposed to Western philosophy and art, to the intellectual positions established by Cartesian Idealism as exploited in the Russia of Tolstoy's day by his spiritual enemies on the authority of their own *intellectual autonomy*, such authority as found in the writings of Hegel, Locke, Kant, Schopenhauer, Nietzsche, Marx. In Tolstoy's rather peculiar understanding of Marx, he implies as his conclusion that Marx is a capitalist in proletarian clothing, his disciples intent on concentrating property and capital "in the hands of a small number of owners." Thus forewarned, one might say, a clever Lenin will carefully enlarge the gulf between the revolutionary and the capitalist-landowner few. Clever in that thereby Lenin gains the control Tolstoy speaks of – the control of *power* over all through the disoriented "spiritual consciousness" which Tolstoy champions, subverting it through a "science" devoted to programmatic control in "arranging the lives of people" as Tolstoy requires. That is Lenin's version of the forced "unity of mankind" – to a religious materialism.

As Gorky suggests, evident in his heated conversations with Tolstoy – conversations Tolstoy may well remember in his castigation of "Marxists" as hidden capitalists – all this manipulation of science and art by Tolstoy is in the name of a spiritual consciousness universal, at the center of which sits the consciousness of Tolstoy as the God of a universal solvency of mankind into an undifferentiated union of "brotherhood." And all this, more deeply, is the strategy of a haunted consciousness who goes in terror of death all his life, tending to reject life in its slow ablution as death's slave – as if life were the disguise worn by Father Death Himself. As Dostoyevsky might well have it (Dostoyevsky uneasy with the Tolstoy of the "tracts"), Tolstoy proves an Inquisitor of life, held to be a Grand Inquisitor by an increasingly sentimentalized "spiritual consciousness" which has almost overwhelmed our own century in its actual destruction of human beings. One hopes that destruction could but horrify Tolstoy were he witness to it. And we may wish to believe that by such recognition he would relocate and intensify his sense of guilt, but in a reality he fanatically denied: that potential to evil implicit in free will, whether one be peasant or tsar.

Tolstoy, we have suggested, in pursuit of the roots of that self-guilt which is always threatening him with despair, comes to conclude as its cause his own actual existence as an *embodied* intellect. He is never at ease with intellect, though

gifted extraordinarily, and he is increasingly discomforted by
the body. Nor is he ever to find an intellectual accommodation sufficient to make acceptable to him his actual circumstances as incarnate consciousness – an *innatured* soul.
Indeed, the actuality of his own existence – an undeniable
existence – seemed more and more evidence to him of personal culpability, beyond redemption because of the sheer
actuality of his own existence. His major sin, in this perspective, is that he exists at all. Such tracts as his "Confession," his
"Religion and Morality" and "The Law of Love and the Law
of Violence," evidence this fear as his dark secret. And so
logic itself must be discredited in a defense against despair,
these given confused circumstances to this consciousness.
Otherwise, logic by extrapolation would require that he reject
actual existence by suicide. On more than one occasion, that
prospect looms before him, a dark necessity he presents with
compelling drama in the character of Levin of *Anna Karenina*.
Indeed, suicide may have been the unnamed temptation to
him on that dark night at Arzamus, his description of that
experience emblematic of his desperation in being alone.
What a confusing terror to confront at that moment. He is
exultantly in love with Sonya; and suddenly he is the talk of
all Russia as his *War and Peace* is reaching the end of its seri-
alization.

The next "logical" necessity short of suicide, following
from his intent to reject his existential reality as a person in
pursuit of expurgation of his haunting guilt, is an Albigensian
response to the world, specifically to that little world entrap-
ping his consciousness, his own body. He is seriously inclined
to self-castration. He can never make that move against his
tormenting body, but he argues passionately for it, as he did
to the dying Chekhov. It becomes imperative to him in this
state of mind that he find good reason to reject logic. But the
trap becomes that to do so he must reject reason itself. And so
reason is argued a man-created devil to consciousness. He
stews in the last four decades of his life in uncertainties,
exploding in passions of rhetoric against human nature itself

as unnatural, as if that given nature were a curse conjured by reason rather than a divine gift. Thus the God of that Orthodox Church, which itself becomes his targeted enemy in the local world, becomes his proximate antagonist. That wry and somewhat bitter Maxim Gorky discovered as much of Tolstoy, expressing the discovery with a sarcastic irony worthy of Tolstoy himself, such as that of Tolstoy's denunciations of the "Christian church" as opposed to his "true Christianity" which Tolstoy invents to his purposes. Gorky sees Tolstoy in his self-appointed role as true prophet to be only an "arrogant aristocrat" parading in a "stage costume of *muzhik* beard and rumpled blouse," treating all persons in his proximity with "the authoritarianism of a provincial governor." "I do not like his idea of God," says Gorky. "It is a part of Count Leo Tolstoy and not God." But in respect to Tolstoy's popularity out of this deportment, as put by Alexis Suvorin of the *New Times,* "we have two tsars, Nicholas and Leo Tolstoy." It is a position Tolstoy has achieved in enlisting the masses in his high sincerity which will not escape Lenin's clever recognitions of the strategy as a means to a pool of power to be exploited.

vi

Gorky does not see in Tolstoy what one might well see in him: a modern version of Dostoyevsky's Grand Inquisitor, defending as the only absolute salvation a recovery as a simply natural child, uncorrupted by thought and perhaps even by consciousness. As such a nature, one is dissolved into *feeling,* freed of logic and reason. Dostoyevsky himself would more probably see in this Tolstoy, not a possession by the diabolic, by a Grand Inquisitor, but simply Gorky's provincial governor. For it is as if Tolstoy were possessed by a much lesser petty devil like that one in *The Brothers Karamazov* who, more than Ivan Karamazov's Grand Inquisitor, drives Ivan to the brink of madness by his very pettiness. That minor devil proves Ivan's Grand Inquisitor revealed to him as natural, worldly, petty man. What wonder that the old man Tolstoy, in flight from all those who love him and who fought with the pettiness of a family squabble to exercise possession of him in his last days – what wonder that Tolstoy should have very much on his mind Dostoyevsky's *Brothers Karamazov*?

Fleeing in the night, he takes little with him, but he does take the opening books of that novel. He writes anxiously to his loyal "Tolstoyean" daughter, Sasha, requesting "the second volume of *The Brothers Karamazov.*" This, on his flight toward the oblivion of death. What did Dostoyevsky know about the terror of diabolic possession that he, Tolstoy, might not have seen? About devils grand and devils petty – the Devil operative under the old dispensations of Rome on the one hand and on the other that anonymous petty devil of the new dispensation of Modernism which had been engineered through science and philosophy by such bright intellects as Ivan Karamazov himself out of Descartes and Kant? In the name of justice and humanity of course. Possession is a terror when encountered on the brink of the final things to a mortal man. For Tolstoy in his wayside railroad station, among his last spoken words are these: "What about the *muzhiks*? How do the *muzhiks* die?"

But before that final question there was the question of art, to which calling and often despite himself, he had given much of his life. What about the *muzhiks* and art, then? What of the innocent (because unlettered) peasant who might stand before whatever object pretending to be art? Certainly that precursor of French Symbolism, now the rage of the sophisticated to the extent that there was talk of a monument to him to be raised in Paris, could only baffle the only true judge of art, that unlettered peasant. Baudelaire, that is, might present himself (as he himself said) as the poet of the "religious intoxication of the great cities" and as such prove fascinating to Tolstoy's "city mob." For they are easily fascinated precisely, Tolstoy says, because that wily French poet (as evidenced by Baudelaire's little poems in prose and by the "intentional obscurity" of those more formal poems of *Flowers of Evil*) lacks any *feelings* truly expressed. Instead, he writes poems "with deliberate originality and absurdity" and cannot be understood "without some effort – an effort seldom rewarded." Many of the poems, indeed, are "entirely incomprehensible," in response to which (assuming they might be available to the unlettered peasant) that peasant would react with incredulity and perhaps with disgust, as Tolstoy himself reacted to the Wagnerian production of the *Ring of the Nibelungen.* The *Flowers of Evil* are a scandal to art, and in Verlaine and Mallermé the scandal but deepens.

One wonders that Tolstoy, who on the evidence of his *What Is Art?* did prodigious readings in the literature of Italy, France, England, and America, fails to be struck by that theme most central to Baudelaire's work, the evil which Tolstoy himself sees festering in the hated city of man. One regrets that he did not notice more carefully, for instance, a preface Baudelaire prepares for those poems. Dostoyevsky would certainly have noticed it: the fact that the poet's concern is for an evil in that city world which that world denies by denying the existence of evil. That denial, says Baudelaire, is evidence of the Devil's shrewdest strategy in our modern world. For Satan has convinced us that he does not exist. That strategy has opened our world for conquest by petty devils such as Ivan Karamazov discovers to have possessed him through a "higher" Nihilism intellectually self-imposed in the name of humanity itself. If Satan does not exist, what then of evil? That is the haunting ambiance of Baudelaire's poetry.

For Tolstoy, to the contrary of both Baudelaire and Dostoyevsky, evil lies not in the heart of man as willfully opening consciousness to such a possession. Evil lies rather in that seeming good, creation itself, as the essence of existential reality. Evil is of the very nature of the world. And the most proximate threat of that evil is for Tolstoy, again, his own body. It is in an attempted rescue of himself through becoming *muzhik* that he would become a figure of the suffering Christ, though he would deny divinity to that Incarnation at Bethlehem. The suffering primarily to be endured is the curse of his mortal body. In the face of this dilemma, then, where suffering can only be anticipated as overcome by death, he turns from good and evil, not by transcending it as would Nietzsche in moving "beyond" that dilemma in a willed superiority to existence, but in an anticlimactic direction: a concentrated concern for good art as opposed to bad art. That is one direction perhaps whereby he may avoid the funda- mentalist observation of Baudelaire which indicts modern man as the dupe of a clever Satan.

In pursuit of distinction between good and bad art as reg- istered by feelings in response to a work, then, Tolstoy sum- mons a recent personal experience (in Chapter XIV) worth our dwelling upon. Returning home from a stroll in "a depressed state of mind," he happens upon "loud singing of a large circle of peasant women. . . . This singing, with shouts and banging on scythes, expressed such a definite feeling of joy, cheerfulness, energy, that without noticing it I became infected by it," becoming cheerful despite himself. The singing was a celebration by the peasants of his daughter's visit, she recently married. That experience Tolstoy then relates to a performance on that "very evening" by a famous musician, especially of "Beethoven's sonata Opus 101." What he recalls experiencing with Beethoven yields a decidedly dif- ferent feeling from that of the true art of the peasant women. He is baffled by the Beethoven sonata. Now Beethoven was among Tolstoy's favorite artists, though not the later Beethoven. Tolstoy admits that, as if one of the "city mob," he had primed himself for a long time to respond favorably to "these formless improvisations which make up the content of the works of Beethoven's late period." In reflection (dare we suggest Tolstoy *thought about, analyzed, reasoned* about the dif- ference in his response?) he concluded that insofar as he was moved by the music he was moved by a "certain vague and almost morbid excitement . . . which I had artificially called up in myself." That is a sure indication that the music was not true art, in contrast to that of the peasant women at their loud singing and clashing of scythes.

Perhaps this is the same occasion well documented by Henri Troyet in his *Tolstoy*, of a performance of Beethoven in July of 1887 when the Tolstoy children arranged a concert at the estate Yasnanya Polyana performed by a visitor from the Moscow Conservatory of Music. At that family gathering Beethoven's "Kreutzer Sonata" was featured. What is reported by those present was that Tolstoy was moved to tears by the performance. His wife Sonya recorded that Tolstoy later that evening proved, in the privacy of their bedroom, to have become "the affectionate and tender Lyovochka of old." A few weeks later, Sonya discovered herself once more pregnant, but a few weeks later, on celebrating their silver wedding anniversary, Tolstoy recorded of that celebration in his own diary that night: "It could have been better!" Soon after, hearing the Beethoven sonata once more in Moscow, Tolstoy proposed that each of those present should give witness of the feeling the music had infected him with. He himself would write a story to be read by an actor (presumably one among those at the occasion). The story would be read before a painting by an artist in testimony of his own feelings out of hearing the concert. An elaborate party game, but it was more than a game for Tolstoy, whose story is the famous (and to his wife Sonya both famous and infamous) "The Kreutzer Sonata" (1889).

The story when written proves an indictment of marriage and of the family, stirring in Tolstoy grave arguments which are put more directly in letters and conversations against conjugal union. Indeed, conjugal abstinence is what is required at least. What Tolstoy means, says Troyet, is that "in order to live in accordance with God's word [see Matthew: 19:12] it was necessary, if not actually to mutilate oneself, at least to forget that one had an instrument for sex." This is the spiritual position of that "affectionate and tender Lyovochka" who had gotten Sonya with child out of feelings (presumably) roused by Beethoven. Beethoven in *What Is Art?* becomes an illustration of the false artist. Thus at sixty, Tolstoy had gotten Sonya with child for the thirteenth time. Meanwhile, the famous (infamous) story once completed, Sonya copied it out, as she did all his work, entering in her diary that she did so cursing and weeping. For she finds herself in the story and in life itself "the fly buzzing in the spider's web and the spider is sucking my blood." But that recognition is not to be the end of her humiliation.

It is Sonya who must go to Petersburg in 1891 to seek permission of the censors at the Court of the Tsar for the publication of the story, a story in which she can only be seen as an evil presence to the protagonist because she is both wife and mother. The whole world, on its publication (so she believes), must reach that conclusion. She must make the humiliating, pleading pilgrimage because Tolstoy has given away all claims to royalty for his works. But Sonya as wife and mother is yet charged with maintaining the estate, which Tolstoy has handed over to the ravenous family – in his estimate of his spiritual peril by that family. As the greatest world writer, Tolstoy draws a steady siege upon his household in visitings by pilgrims from around the world, who by that local hospitality must be fed and housed. There is also the large family and its retainers as well, who must be cared for by this mother of the tribe of Tolstoys. Meanwhile, she must copy and recopy tracts and stories. (She is said to have copied out *War and Peace* four times.) What keeps her going is her own discipleship to Tolstoy as artist, for she never wavers in her belief that Tolstoy is a great genius. And further sustaining her, she never wavers in her discipline as Orthodox Christian. His being a great writer is a matter aside from his being her husband and the father of their children, the spider sucking her blood.

In the final decade of last century, Tolstoy was confident – with the "authoritarianism of a provincial governor" – that he knew the answer to the question of what the *muzhik* thought of art. Thus in *What Is Art?* he gives us an absolute answer with a passionate rhetoric mimicking reason. He writes art criticism against art criticism. It is difficult, he says, for anyone to admit that the judgment on "which they have arranged

their entire life" could "be wrong." And yet, "if we once recognize as true that art is a human activity by means of which
some people convey their feelings to others, and is not the
service of beauty, the manifestation of an idea, and so on, then
it must needs be admitted." (In a note to his text, concerning
the importance of the "content" of art as being his version of
Christianity, he says "I must note . . . that I rank my own artistic works on the side of bad art, except for the story "God Sees
the Truth.") As for the art of the tract itself, the fierceness of
his answer to the question leads to a tedious repetitiveness,
though somewhat alleviated by passion, a fireworks of anger,
along the way. It is a passion necessary to defend himself
against that despair which must follow his conclusion that he
himself has failed as artist. He is fanatical, out of a necessity
to keep at bay the haunting conclusion that his only honor-
able recourse would be to blow out his brains. And again,
Dostoyevsky is himself acutely attuned to this relation of dislocated guilt, a theme repeatedly present in his fiction,
momentarily tempting that same final solution. Dostoyevsky
is almost addicted to deathbed scenes in his fictions. Suicide
is a repeated event, usually preceded by agonizing guilt in
characters whose logic leads them to oblivion as the only
solution – those lacking the courage of endurance in suffering
guilt like Dostoyevsky's heroes but more often than not hero-
ines.

Short of that spectacular solution, *feeling* itself (the center
for Tolstoy's principle to art) may delay a final conclusion.
But what is necessary, he says, is the artist's "sincerity" of
feeling so that art sincerely felt into existence by the artist will
"infect" others. Drawing toward this conclusion, after many
insistent uses of the term *feeling* as the necessary evidence of
a desired "infection" engendering "religion," Tolstoy puts the
point yet once more in Chapter XV: "*The stronger the infection,
the better the art, regardless of its content – that is, independently
of the worth of the feeling it conveys.*" For if the feeling is overwhelming, all reflection and thought become obviated and
one's consciousness becomes thereby melded into a forgetfulness

in a Kantian universal consciousness, to which is added by
his argument the vagueness of Hindu Brahmanism, a "feeling" of the "Self" as God. That is one way to move "beyond
good and evil." The worth of the feeling can only be engaged
by thought through reason, and reason must be avoided. That
is why one must become *muzhik*, "a man of unperverted taste,
a labouring man, not a city-dweller."

Such a creature will recognize a true work of art, because
for him there occurs an instinctive response of feeling to the
sincere feeling of the artist. It is a response "as easy as it is for
an animal with an unspoiled scent to find . . . the one it
needs." Such a man of the people therefore may be "infected"
by feeling made artful by the artist, who must be himself a
man of the people. But "reasoning and examination" can only
be an unwanted vaccination killing feeling. Yet that is the
very vaccination propounded as necessary by the intelligentsia, the "big-city mob," as witnessed by the flood of
books on aesthetics. Through the "infection" of "feeling," if
one is innocent of such a vaccination, we will necessarily
"merge our souls with another's" [that of the "sincere"
artist's], and that "constitutes the essence of art." And so at
last, by the logic of his argument he denies logic on principle.
For Tolstoy, true art is possible only to the "simple, unperverted working people." The true artist himself can only be
true if he is one of them, "a man of the people." If this be so,
where does it leave Tolstoy as artist? Unavoidably, he must
conclude himself as artist doomed to false art, given his property and education. He sees himself as coming closest to the
recovery he desires in only one of his works, that little-known
story of his, "God Sees the Truth." Meanwhile he must surrender all copyright, divest himself of all property, in an act of
expiation regardless of its effect upon the ever-faithful Sonya.

If the "aim of art is to infect people with a [sincere] feeling
experienced by the artist," that constant metaphor *infect*
seems intended to name a spontaneity of feeling consonant
with the poet's spontaneous – "sincere" – feeling. But the
problem, carefully avoided by Tolstoy, is the one T. S. Eliot

runs headlong into in his own attempt to escape entrapment as false artist – the problem Eliot speaks of as the necessity to the artist in his making, through selectivity: a reasoned choosing of sufficient "objective correlatives." Eliot gives us a formula definition of the "objective correlative" out of chemical science, a definition which would horrify Tolstoy and which Eliot himself will come to see as insufficient to the very real problem of art's service to a communal participation. And Eliot will later, unlike Tolstoy, turn to the Church to discover the true grounding of images in creation as creation, rather than in science's deductions from that reality. He turns to an orthodox understanding of human nature which denies the Manichaean position Tolstoy insists upon. Eliot has said in his essay on "Hamlet and His Problems" (1919), "The only way of expressing emotion [Tolstoy's "feeling"?] in the form of art is by finding an 'objective correlative' . . . a set of objects, a situation, a chain of events which shall be the formula of that *particular* emotion; such that when the external facts, which must terminate in sensory experience, are given, the emotion is immediately evoked."

Tolstoy to the contrary is insistent that the particular feeling must be sincerely engaged and expressed by the artist without thinking on such matters as the appropriateness of objective correlatives. But as we have argued, what Tolstoy cannot escape, try though he may, is that *feelings* involve inescapably "sensory experience." That is the curse of art to Tolstoy which he never escapes, the curse of his own body and its senses as he sees it. Eliot, long before he comes to understand his own argument in its most profound theological dimension, has pointed to the problem fundamental in Tolstoy's own aesthetics, a problem deeper than aesthetics can resolve by the "sciences" of theology and philosophy in subvention of the curse of the body and its senses. And so Eliot, long before he comes himself to understand his own arguments concerning the decay of art in the modern world as profoundly related to theological questions, pointed to the problem already fundamental in Tolstoy's advocacy of religious aesthetics. It is a problem to which the "sciences" of theology and philosophy as propounded by Tolstoy are insufficient. We have suffered in English poetry, Eliot says in his essay in rescue of the English Metaphysical poets (just before his own dramatization of intellectual collapse called *The Waste Land*) – we have suffered a "dissociation of sensibilities," a dissociation for Eliot "aggravated by the influence of the two most powerful poets of the [17th] century, Milton and Dryden." It is a dissociation conspicuous in its effects in the rise of Romanticism, in which "while the language became more refined, the feeling became more crude." The argument might well be Tolstoy's, until we come to the cause of that disparity as Eliot sees it: the separation of thought and feeling effects a dissociation from which the poet must recover. It is a recovery not to be made by an elevation of feeling over thought.

Not since Milton and Dryden, we are saying, but since Cartesian dislocations of intellect there grows this dissociation. For out of that separation, whereby "science" elects as its province thought and "art" elects feeling, in opposition to each other increasingly – scientist or poet – there comes to be established as article of faith the supremacy of intellect over all else as itself autonomous, whether it advocate as primary either thought or feeling. In that new faith, intellect separates itself increasingly from both nature and nature's God, with a conspicuous struggle in the Romantic poet to recover from his dislocation. For that poet, it seems a problem unlikely to be resolved by any appeal to aesthetics as a "science." As for Eliot, he turns toward orthodoxy, declaring an orthodox belief necessary if there is to be any recovery of intellect to nature and history, to "tradition." In orthodoxy lies the necessary enlargement of a tradition recovered from mere feeling through thought, through a metaphysics restoring sensibilities to intellect itself in the ordinate relation of thought to feeling. (That is the position Eliot dramatizes in his "Ash-Wednesday.")

There is in Tolstoy at least an implicit recognition of this dissociation as having occurred. His becomes an attempt at recovery through a program whereby science's thought is translated by art's feeling. But that is hardly a restoration of thought to feeling, though there is a reassociation, thus prescribing to all men "how human life should be arranged," no doubt to be defined in detail by joint committee. In that attempt, of course, Tolstoy is adamant in rejecting tradition, mythology, metaphysics, history as evidences of a bondage to the past in this present moment of "people and society." As for intellect, it must reject reason, logic, analysis, examination, reflection and the like, submitting only to the "sincerity" of "feeling" in this moment. That is the necessary means to an amalgamation of all mankind into what he declares to be the only religion acceptable, that "religious consciousness" which he identifies as the "brotherhood of man," to be made manifest in the world in a uniting of "all people into a socialist state or commune . . . a world federation." *Brotherhood* in Tolstoy is an *idea*, for which at times he uses another term, in a translation influenced by Eastern thought. *Brotherhood* perfected is *God*.

vii

If, from what we have seen of Tolstoy in his concern to establish the brotherhood of man in history, we feel uncomfortable with him as philosopher and theologian – with his wisdom in riddling common experiences and relating those experiences to first causes – what are we to make of him in this dimension of his presence to us in a defense of art? Of one judgment, we tend to be held to a common consent: he is a great artist, imitating persuasively the actions of human nature in the confused world of our Modernist circumstances. If he does not at last prove tragedian, he certainly moves us by that pathos which is so typical of art since the dominance of the Modernist dogmas which establish man as autonomous intellect. For pathos is the feeling, the effect, man suffers increasingly in consequence of his alienation from both nature and community. In his person as artist, turning from his art to a principle concern for that alienation, a concern for a "brotherhood of man" to be directed by his own version of science, through those directions translated to feeling by the artist, how shall we characterize Tolstoy's intellectual legacy?

In Leo Strauss's *Natural Right and History*, perhaps we are provided some purchase upon Tolstoy's thought, for despite his repugnance to thought Tolstoy thinks and thinks and thinks. We might consider him, then, under a rubric Strauss develops, suggesting him *historicist* whenever he falls from his gifts as artist. From the time of *War and Peace*, Tolstoy wrestles with the problem of history as it relates to art, never finally escaping an infection of himself as thinker by his early devotions to Hegel, whom he nevertheless struggles to exorcise from both his thought and feeling. Flaubert in a letter to Turgenev praises *War and Peace* very highly, though he laments that such a great work is flawed by speculative essays on history. (Turgenev shared the letter with Tolstoy.) But it is not history at last which proves the problem to Tolstoy's speculative concerns for the brotherhood of man. It is rather Tolstoy's uneasy sense – intuition – that philosophy alone might resolve the relation of history and art in respect to community within the realities of the human condition. But he must reject philosophy as deceptive in that it requires reason as the principle to any action in words.

Still, he does not realize how deeply he has been "infected" in his thought by Hegel, however much he attempts the exorcism of Hegelian thought from his "feelings," along with any other philosophical thought which is inimical to mere "feelings." He is left in a condition of mind which that astute analyst of the Modernist mind, Leo Strauss, engages in his *Natural Right and History*. Through Strauss's observations, then, we may see the Hegelian presence in Tolstoy's "conclusion" to *What Is Art?* Tolstoy would declare, for instance, that only the present state of the people is acceptable as a "spiritual" ground for progress toward brotherhood in the world.

Strauss remarks that "Hegel had taught that every philosophy is the conceptual expression of the spirit of its time," which idea Tolstoy attempts to transfer to a spiritual level, away from the philosophical concerns of Hegel. But in doing so, he is caught in the contradiction Strauss observes of Hegel as philosopher. For Hegel, "maintained the absolute truth of his own system of philosophy by ascribing absolute character to his own time; he assumed that his own time was the end of history and hence the absolute moment." Rather than philosophy's triumph in an act of revelation of the end of history, Hegel succeeds only in unleashing upon the intellectual community that most various creature, ideology, each of which species supposes itself bearer of a gnostic truth, its own metaphysics of the "end of history." Among these increasingly random erosions of philosophy, the one that rises in the nineteenth century and comes to dominate the twentieth, according to Strauss, is "historicism." It is an intellectual position amenable to Tolstoy because it rejects philosophy itself, though it does so by assuming the Hegelian philosophical position of its own absoluteness, certified to it because this present moment is the latest moment of history, superseding thereby all authority that is past.

"The historicist contention," says Strauss "can be reduced to the assertion that natural right is impossible because philosophy in the full sense of the term is impossible." From the perspective of historicism, "What is called the 'experience of history' is a bird's-eye view of the history of thought, as that history came to be seen under the combined influence of the belief in necessary progress (or the impossibility of returning to the thought of the past) and of the belief in the supreme value of diversity or uniqueness (or of the equal rights of all epochs or civilizations)." In this respect, Tolstoy is himself devoted to an inclusive "multiculturalism," but it is of a species which demands the obliteration by each individual of all differentiating characteristics of his culture. If Dostoyevsky to the contrary sees the "*Russian* soul" as the only possible rescue of mankind from spiritual collapse,

Tolstoy concedes only a necessity to rescue the *soul*, which he translates to a vague "brotherhood of man," within which brotherhood all particularity is to be dissolved. He rejects his disciple Gandhi, for instance, because Gandhi will not deny his own "Indianness."

In listening to Tolstoy in his "Conclusion," we hear the historicist whom Strauss examines as ideologue, whose faith he calls *historicism*. Strauss observes that "Historicism asserts that all human thoughts or beliefs are historical, and hence deservedly destined to perish." The flaw: "historicism itself is a human thought; hence historicism can be of only temporary validity, or it cannot be simply true." But "Historicism thrives on the fact that it inconsistently exempts itself from its own verdict about human thought [*pace* Hegel]." And so a philosopher, Strauss, must conclude that the "historicist thesis is self-contradictory or absurd." For "We cannot see the historical character of 'all' thought . . . without transcending history, without grasping something trans-historical." And here lies a frustrating circumstance to Tolstoyean thought. For Tolstoy resolutely rejects the transcendent, at last, as he rejects history itself as dead thought, leaving him only with nature. But then nature proves for him again and again the most subtle of all his enemies, holding his "feeling" hostage through the body.

If we consider Tolstoy in his position as historicist, we might wonder whether for him history does not appear increasingly the buried, poisonous tentacles of nature freed to destructions of "the brotherhood of man" by a reason which is regardless of feeling. It is from this position that he might well be inclined to that adaptation of Hegelian thought, whereby he concludes that this present moment, in which humanity finds itself beleaguered by nature and history, is the moment from which a rescue is possible, but only by a rejection of nature and nature's history. Thus that insistence on departing from "a reasonable religious world view that corresponds to our time," a view to be served by "true science" and made manifest in present mankind through the services of "true art" through its infections of mankind by "pure feeling."

We find the seed of this final position already planted in his "Epilogue" to *War and Peace*, his long (overlong, in Flaubert's judgment) engagement of the problem of history. In his opening words (Part I) he declares that the "subject of history is the life of nations and of mankind," whereby the historian is undertaking the "impossible" in describing "the life of a single people much less that of mankind." Given that will is as "subject to laws" as a stone to gravity and so cannot be declared "free," what then? For reason presuming to present "life" must conclude that "the concept of freedom appears as a meaningless contradiction." The historian no less than Napoleon is a slave to deterministic history. Tolstoy is still able to affirm nevertheless that "Man is the creation of an omniscient, omnipotent, and infinitely good God." But if reason is right, then man is a determined creature, contradictory in his nature to the cause of that nature, a "good God." Therefore reason can only be suspect.

In his speculative "Epilogue," Tolstoy is attempting to come to terms with such presences among us as Napoleon in particular, who has figured large in that great novel. But all that we know of Napoleon and all that our reason can make of him in respect to his history and his effect upon peoples – the light of history upon ultimate ends as possessed by reason through knowledge – is insufficient. We must, then, renounce "the claim of knowledge of an ultimate aim," whereupon "we shall clearly see" that a Napoleon is "adapted down to the smallest detail to the purpose [he] had to fulfill. . . ." He is the perfected instrument of nature revealed in the moment, determined down to the "smallest detail" to his purpose in this moment of power whose source is nature. "*Chance,* millions of *chances,* give him power. . . ."

It will follow from such thought, as it eventually does for Tolstoy, that the only defense of free will lies in a rejection of knowledge, of history, of nature, with an ultimate dependence placed in *feeling* thus freed from reason itself. For "The higher the human intellect rises in the revelation of these purposes" in a nature engendering history, "the more obvious it becomes that the ultimate purpose of mankind is beyond our comprehension." That ultimate purpose will be increasingly declared by Tolstoy as self-elected prophet to be the "brotherhood of man," to be accomplished by feeling freed of any thought governed by reason.

In the issue, then, Tolstoy's circumstances as thinker prove harbinger of pathos, out of that widening gulf between consciousness and nature (and nature's history) on the one hand, and between consciousness and its Causing God on the other. It will leave that consciousness isolated in itself as the only godhead acceptable to itself, and that can but effect a depth of pathos in relation to "ultimate aim" bordering on despair. Given the mind as thus haunted by history (history itself concluded nature's minion), nature's empowered slave is a sum of chance, Napoleon in sum an image of man as determined. The threat for Tolstoy is the enslavement of his own will in this present "historical" moment of consciousness in nature. Most especially this includes Tolstoy's enslavement by his own personal history. And so he turns in a fierce antipathy, against all philosophy and theology antecedent to his own present moment, and against his own history as *this* person. He rejects the theology of the Orthodox Church. He rejects philosophy, which for him means almost exclusively that Western philosophy associated with the names of Descartes, Hegel, Marx, and so on. But in doing so he proves not a "true historian" of himself or of his people, but only a historicist, forced to accept that all human thought and belief antecedent to his own moment is dead history to be dismissed out of hand. The irony becomes that he cannot dismiss it out of his own mind, so that there continues in him the influence of those Western philosophers who for awhile seemed "enlightened" to him. Nor does he escape lingering effects from his Orthodox upbringing, an evidence of which is his evolving substitute sacramental deportment – his vegetarianism, his robes of the *muzhik*. An additional irony: as historicist, he is left with progress as a primary principle, however variously progress may be defined by other historicists. In the interest of that progress there is nevertheless one common consent among the historicists, recalling us to Tolstoy and his "Conclusion." There is required for progress, "a fusion of science and the arts together with the unlimited and uncontrolled progress of technology," as Strauss observes.

That, as Tolstoy recognized even as he accepts it, is a decided danger, so that in his own argument for such a fusion, he attempts to counter technology itself, as in his advocating the simple man's eating an egg from a hen he has raised, an apple from a tree on his own spot of land. Such are the "natural" actions necessary to a brotherhood of man. Even if but intuitively, Tolstoy recognizes the danger Strauss enunciates as resulting from this fusing of art and science toward technological progress, the "universal and perpetual tyranny" which is "a serious possibility." The universalism Tolstoy attempts to substitute instead is the "brotherhood of man." That such was a forlorn hope, once he had insistently rejected the relation of the transcendent to the immanent, seems his last haunting terror, indistinguishable from death as he comes to the edge of death itself. This is hinted at on his flight from home and family (or so I contend) by his first visiting the monastery earlier visited by Dostoyevsky in preparing to write *The Brothers Karamazov*. On that visit, Tolstoy could not find the *staretz* he wished to see – the current "Father Zossima." And so he launches forth by means of that new creature of technology, the train, uncertain of destination. His anxious request just before his death is that his daughter get to him the last books of Dostoyevsky's novel, in which the historicist as nihilist, Ivan Karamazov, has a dark night of the soul, an encounter with that petty devil who will lead Ivan to conclude that as rational Nihilist he is (as he says to Alyosha) a "Romantic."

Although Leo Strauss in his *Natural Right and History* nowhere mentions Tolstoy, one of his observations along the way is resonant to our concerns: "The contemporary rejection of natural rights leads to nihilism – nay, it is identical with nihilism," though Strauss would be reluctant to accept our own conclusion concerning the rejection of the doctrine called natural rights. That because Strauss's version of this doctrine is the classical, not the orthodox Thomistic one. The orthodox position one finds in John Paul II's explication of it in *The Splendor of Truth*, in an attack on Modernist denials. From our perspective, the rejection of the orthodox doctrine of natural rights denies to intellect its only true ground in which the immanent may be reconciled to the transcendent. From that orthodox position, a metaphysical argument must address the mystery of that moment of history called the Incarnation, in which moment history itself is rescued from historicism beyond those attempts of rescue which might be termed the classical doctrine of natural rights. It is that mystery to which Strauss, welcomed ally in opposition to Modernist erosions of intellect itself, cannot himself reach any accommodation, so that his welcomed recovery of classical natural rights is an elementary necessity to a fuller recovery and does not prove at last sufficient in itself. As for this mystery of the Incarnation, we find that Tolstoy early and repeatedly rejects both philosophy and mystery, both necessary to a metaphysical vision of the true nature of any "brotherhood of man." He does so especially in rejecting the Incarnation, in his attempt to establish his own Christianity, from which he has fiercely exorcised Christ, in whose stead at last he stands. That was Gorky's cutting conclusion.

Seeing the Country of Reality: A Preliminary

Here we do not intend an extended engagement of the orthodox doctrine of natural law as a preamble to our concern for an orthodox view of beauty, our concluding concern. Nevertheless, beauty contributes significantly in relation to natural law to our journey through creation, our faring as *homo viator*. While in that country we as a "consciousness" encounter "things." And in the response of consciousness to encounter of created things – summed cumulatively as experience – beauty in things affects our deportment toward the world in which we journey. Now the gift to intellect called *natural law* is a gift to consciousness whereby it participates in knowing the limits of the being of things within the orders of creation, according to intellect's own limits. Intellect's consent to an extrinsic ordering, independent of Modernism's presumption of its own causal power, prepares intellect to respond to the beauty of things. For beauty is consequent upon the *created* limits of things, affecting consciousness with a delight – a pleasure – in the being of things – in *a* thing's being the thing it *is*.

There is a further, though secondary, concern in our introducing this proper deportment of intellect to the realities of things, yielding the concepts of *natural right* or *natural law*. In our reaction to the perversions of things made by intellect in the name of beauty, contrary to natural law – distortions of the truth of things in the interest of appetitive ends as the finality to our journeying – we may welcome allies also opposing that distortion. But in the ensuing confederation of a common resistance, it is also necessary to know the limits of that very confederation. Thus, if we speak of a *classical* concept of natural rights, as does Leo Strauss, and of an *orthodox* Christian concept of natural law, as does Thomas Aquinas, we require discretion in respect to differences between them, lest by ignoring internal differences among confederate allies our common strategies of resistance to a common antagonist become problematic. Meanwhile the Modernist's reduction of natural rights is akin to his reduction of beauty itself. For Modernism, as we argue, has declared creation's limit to be subservient to autonomous intellect. That intellect presumes to exercise "rights" over "nature," to appetitive ends – the ultimate limit of vision to that Modernist position. Tolstoy's attack on this inclination as reflected in Modernist aesthetics, then, is highly justified. It is his consequent dislocation of his argument from ultimate ends, through his own reductionist arguments about reality (his Manichaeanism), which becomes the problem.

We are concerned for a moment, then, to clarify the limits of alliance between *classical* natural rights and *orthodox* natural rights, as understood respectively by Leo Strauss and Etienne Gilson or Jacques Maritain out of Thomas Aquinas. In one of his formulations, *Summa Theologiae*, I–II, q 91, a. 2, Thomas says, "Among all others, the rational creature is subject to divine providence in the most excellent way, insofar as it partakes of a share of providence, being provident both for itself and for others. Thus it has a share of the Eternal Reason, whereby it has a natural inclination to its proper act and end. This participation of the eternal law in the rational creature is called natural law." There is a quite different understanding in the concepts, as of their ultimate service to man's ultimate ends, consequent upon the differences between these positions. The point must be recognized, though in an alliance they engage a common antagonist, Modernism. To have some purchase upon difference is to have some measure of alliance, to have some ground in which to reckon, for instance, additional alliances we may find with others in a confederation against Modernism. For thus we identify allies as various from Strauss as the philosopher Eric Voegelin or the poet T. S. Eliot.

We begin, then, by affirming a belief in natural law, affecting natural rights and therefore both civil law and social manners as well. The concept speaks to a reality attendant upon creation itself, independent of intellectual will. This is not merely fancy's idea projected for an intellectual convenience. We further argue that our concern is with what at first may seem at a far remove, our concern for the nature of beauty. But we may find that beauty is both reality and concept, correlative in our active participation as intellectual creatures in God's providence to creation, a participation Thomas speaks of as man's rational participation in the *eternal* law. In its local presence to intellect we call it "natural law." Such was the arresting recognition to the artist Eric Gill when he encountered Thomas's judgment that beauty is "that which when seen pleases." It proved arresting because it so aptly characterized for him the truth of his own experiences as artist, as a maker of things. By that encounter of Thomas's argument, Gill builds his whole life as artist, his testimony of that devotion pointedly evident in the titles to two collections of his essays: *Beauty Looks After Herself* and then a range of selected essays called *It All Goes Together*. It all does go together in the depths of understanding.

And so this brief foray into the intellectual position on natural rights and natural law as traditional concepts in order that we may enlarge our prospects upon beauty. For the concept of beauty requires a metaphysical context. With that concern we may distinguish two traditions, the classical and then the orthodox, which succeeds and envelops the classical concern for natural right, which was fundamentally concerned with the ordering of the political and social body of the *polis*.

We noted the classical as the position Leo Strauss advances against Modernist manipulations of natural rights. For by that manipulation, served by an empirical science divorced of transcendent dependence, "natural law" becomes summary deduction by abstract analysis, the "law" thus yielded turned to gnostic ends in the interest of reconstituting being itself.

For comparison to Strauss as our ally, we shall use John Paul II as advocate of the orthodox concept. For Strauss the authority of reference is primarily Plato, with lesser dependences on Aristotle. As for the active, participating authority within the political arena of this classical natural law, Strauss depends heavily upon Cicero – as (incidentally) so did our own founders in their moderating toward an emerging antagonistic "Modern Natural Rights." Strauss engages that antagonist as rising with the Enlightenment, gaining power through the French Revolution and then broadly "infecting" the Western world. (Strauss's exploration, indeed, will shed some light on the disquiet felt by some of our Founding Fathers in response to what the French Revolution made of liberty, justice, and fraternity at the close of the 18th century.) One notes that Strauss often cites comparatively Thomas's *Summa Theologiae*. But in doing so he is concerned for a compatibility to the classical model as he adapts Thomas to the classical concept. In his considering the correspondence of Thomas's arguments to the classical doctrine which is primary to Strauss, Strauss carefully dissociates his own position from any implications of a theism in his own doctrine, his classical natural law. His is a faith in classical philosophy over orthodox theology, though he will reject almost angrily any dependence on faith – as he does in correspondence with Voegelin.

To the contrary, John Paul II's uses of Thomas are out of a commitment to that revelation whereby God is made man in order to rescue man. Thus he emphasizes that "*The moral law has its origin in God and always finds its source in him.*" He adds that, by the virtue of natural reason as derived from divine wisdom, man may discover a "*properly human law.*" In

Thomas's words, the natural law "is nothing other than the light of understanding infused in us by God, whereby we understand what must be done and what must be avoided." That understanding defines the limits of natural rights. There is, then, a "rightful autonomy" of the practical reason, John Paul II remarks, in that man possesses in himself his own intellectual law. But since it is a received law – received from his creator – this *"autonomy of reason cannot mean* that reason itself *creates values and moral norms"* (John Paul's emphasis). Human law, then, *depends from* natural law, which depends in and through creation according to God's providence, to be experienced by man as *homo viator*.

As for man as central figure in this relation of law to creation, a relation speaking to his obligations of stewardship in creation, Thomas has put the matter as we have cited him, that by a natural participation in the eternal law man possesses a gift of that participation as intrinsic to his nature as intellectual creature. Thus intellect has a natural inclination to its proper act and end. This participation of the eternal law in the rational creature is called "natural law." As free intellectual agent, intellect by that "natural right" – that is, according to its created nature – is arbiter of natural law in the measure of civil and social order. That is the principle which lies at the heart of man's responsibility to creation as steward.

Important to our concern is the position that the natural law lies *in* the rational creature, enabling his proportionate participation in that eternal law governing existence as created. Man participates by virtue of that most excellent gift to human nature whereby reason itself in intellectual action is in its limited degree participant in Eternal Reason. The autonomy of reason is thus proportionate, being not absolute as the Modernist would have it. It is participatory, let us emphasize, in relation to an incommensurate distinction between the created (the person) and the Creator. And so John Paul II speaks of this orientation of intellect as limited in its autonomy, whereby "man's proper and primordial nature, the 'nature' of the human person,' . . . is *the person himself in the unity of soul*

and body, in the unity of his spiritual and biological inclinations and of all the other specific characteristics necessary for
the pursuit of his end." Put in this manner, there is a considerable difference in respect to natural law or natural rights
between the readings of man's nature by the classical and the
orthodox concepts.

While Leo Strauss might summon Aquinas to the support
of Plato, the orthodox reading of natural rights rather summons Plato to Thomas in some degree, as does Josef Pieper in
his essay on Plato, *"Divine Madness"*: *Plato's Case against
Secular Humanism,* in which Pieper observes correspondences
anticipatory of Thomas in Plato, Thomas's argument yet to be
made in the *Summa Theologiae.* It is a crucial difference, this
between classical and orthodox doctrines of natural rights,
which is put summarily by John Paul II: "The natural law
[thus understood by orthodox principles] does not allow for
any division between freedom and nature," since these are
"harmoniously bound together," and most self-evidently so
in that creature in whom natural rights and natural law guide
natural reason in that conduct of *homo viator* called stewardship. We might suggest, then, that classical natural law may
inevitably yield a heroic Stoicism, such as that of Cicero, but
it cannot conclude in an accommodation of freedom and
nature as reconciled in human nature.

With that prelude, we turn once more to Leo Strauss and
his concern expressed in *Natural Right and History* and here
attempt a summary of his classical concern in relation to the
orthodox concern. We do so, lest our argument be put off its
course by an uncritical alliance with Strauss. With such care,
we shall be the better prepared in our concern for the mystery
of beauty as "that which when seen pleases." In anticipation,
Thomas Aquinas sees a beauty immanent in things in relation
to the essential nature of each thing. Through human reason
he contemplates the wonders of creation as speaking through
the gifts *of* intellect *to* intellect. For that allows fulfillment of
the potential, a concomitant of which is happiness through
the beauty of things. It is we might say (if mindful of proportion-

ate difference in similars) the experience whereby contempla-
tively the person sees the thing in itself and sees that it is
good, as God so "saw" the whole of creation on the seventh
day. Such is a virtue in that gift of participation in Eternal
Reason and Eternal Law which he describes as man's being
subject to "it in the most excellent way," having been created
in the image of God. There is possible, this is to say, a beauty
in that very limit of our existence as created intellectual soul
incarnate – a beauty out of participation as such a creature in
that Divine Beauty of the Creator – proportionate to Divine
Beauty. Should we seek testimony from the poet to such coin-
cident beauty, to Beauty in its ultimate end, the grandest
attempt at its celebration may well be Dante's conclusion to
the *Divine Comedy*, that moment envisioning the "multifoliate
rose."

Meanwhile to our benefit in attempting a recovery of that
way to Beauty, Leo Strauss (especially in his *Natural Right and
History*, 1953) is concerned to rescue the reality of natural
rights from Modernist reductionism, a reductionism practiced through contending philosophies of power in pursuit of
power over being. He remarks, for instance, that "Since the
seventeenth century, philosophy has become a weapon, and
hence an instrument." The reductionism lies, though it lies
variously in schools of contention, in the reduction of history
to present circumstances of convenience in the interest of
proximate ends born of this present moment. By that reductionism, history is made slave to the moment. It becomes a
false traditionalism now some centuries old, a reading of
"history" in justification of current intentionalities. Thus
Strauss on Hegel: "Hegel had taught that every philosophy is
the conceptual expression of the spirit of its time." But that
involves a contradiction all too evident in Hegel's argument
since he yet "maintained the absolute truth of his own system
of philosophy by ascribing absolute character to his own
time." That is what is meant by Hegel's assumption "that his
own time was the end of history and hence the absolute
moment." Meanwhile more radical historicists than Hegel

rise prominently in the nineteenth century, building on the shifting sands of the Hegelian present moment as absolute. They will assert as a beginning in their own end moment that all thoughts and beliefs are merely historical, hence destined to perish. (One of the most diabolical deployments is that of Comte, in his creation of sociology as a Modernist religion.) Hence the irony noted by Strauss: "Historicism thrives on the fact that it inconsistently exempts itself from its own verdict about all human thought."

The inescapable enemy to this Modernist spirit proves implicit in creation itself, whatever the peculiarities of that Modernist spirit or however hard-pressed we may be to oppose that spirit. That enemy is the actual *natural right* measured by created limit circumscribing *right*, since in that actuality of existential reality lies the measure of limit, the actual *proportionate* control of history itself being separate from any intellectual desire for power over nature which presumes an absolute exercise of power in this present moment through self-liberated intellect. Thus Strauss on the historicist: "The historicist contention can be reduced to the assertion that natural right is impossible because philosophy in the full sense of the term is impossible." It is impossible to Modernist philosophy, this is to say, that it confidently judge truth by reality since its faith rests in an inversion, the consequence of unbridling intellectual power presumed a freedom, from which distortion of reality proceeds the imputed authority to intellect as the absolute arbitrator of truth. In accord with whatever degree of power it can manifest in the present moment, it dictates truth. Thus an intention to a presumed end, projected by intellect independent of reality, measures truth at last by intent. And, given the uneasy civil wars within Modernism itself, it becomes a convenience to agree that truth is relative – but not relative to any absolute. In the event, it proves relative to power possessed by factions.

Strauss, then, is concerned to recover natural right as a reality to intellect, beyond any presumed autonomy, and it is with this reality that intellect must come to terms. He opposes, let us say figuratively, a secular angelism though he does so from a secular position which is not itself beyond suspicion as angelism. The natural right he would recover is the classical, not the Christian. In the course of his argument he acknowledges that it is the Christian sense of natural right that has contended most effectively – philosophically speaking – with Modernism in recent centuries, though it has slowly lost ground to various Modernist dogmas of intellectual ideology which have been based in the assumed autonomy of intellect itself. That is a social-political phenomenon observable at mid-century as he writes, observing as he does the current banners of the Modernist position in the academy and in the halls of civil authority, as earlier he could observe it in the political sphere in what some would call a civil war within Modernist ideology itself. The intellectual community of Strauss's moment marches under the banner of "liberalism," against which forces he sets his argument. Thus we find such of his observations as these: "When liberals became impatient of the absolute limits to diversity or individuality that are imposed even by the most liberal version of natural rights, they had to make a choice between natural right and uninhibited cultivation of individuality." As to current circumstances following that choice, especially evident in both the political arena and in the academy consequent to World War II, "Present-day American social science, as far as it is not Roman Catholic social science, is dedicated to the proposition that all men are endowed by the evolutionary process or by a mysterious fate with many kinds of urges and aspirations, but certainly not with natural rights." And some of us (perhaps including John Paul II, judging from his encyclicals) might with the passing of almost fifty years since Strauss's argument, be reluctant to exempt "Roman Catholic social science," particularly as evidenced in our own hemisphere.

So far, then, in the opening of his argument for a recovery of natural right, Strauss appears most welcomed by the Christian ("Roman") defenders of natural rights. Both are concerned with *truth* as independent of mysterious fate, human urges, or instinctive hungers as sufficient to account for those conditions yielding accelerating social and political problems in our century. Those readings of reality contrary to that of Strauss and a few "Romans" can be used to justify power codified by law to order both nature and civil man to an accord with the desires of whatever current master of power – whether he be a "liberal" or "conservative" master as tyrant, whether a Stalin or a Hitler to set an emblematic extreme – by which historic allusion we suggest confusions attendant upon carelessly used terms.

Where Strauss parts company with the Christian advocate of natural rights is in the Christian's going beyond the limits of the classical concept into a metaphysics relating the transcendent and immanent. Strauss sees the ground to the truth of natural right in nature *per se*, a concept he argues discovered by the Greek thinkers and held to by classical Roman activists such as Cicero. It is this *so far and no further* alliance of Strauss with Christian metaphysics which is a cause of that uneasy relation of Strauss to Eric Voegelin at last to which we have alluded, made specific in their argument over the relation of *faith* to *philosophy* in their correspondence. What that means for the Christian natural rights defender is that both he and Strauss share an analytical understanding of the false philosophy of Modernism, seeing a manipulation of philosophy in Modernist arguments becoming both weapon and instrument, forcing ends aptly speculated on by Strauss and rejected by him. For we "are forced to suspect that historicism [as one aspect of the Modernist appropriation of power over man and nature through philosophy] is the guise in which dogmatism likes to appear in our age." And so the most fundamental enemy to Strauss, we begin to discover, is dogmatism itself, so that Modernism in the liberal dogmas of "our age" must be opposed but with a careful recognition of distinction between the allies to that opposition. Again, that was a necessity which Voegelin came to discover, estranging him from Strauss.

Christian natural rights is for Strauss, then, at last a dogma surviving from an earlier age which he cannot accept. What one speculates, concerning Strauss's thought on such matters, is that he must maintain what he sees (believes on faith) is his own absolute intellectual freedom, independent of commitment to any "dogma" by that faith lest his intellectual integrity be thereby compromised. For him the "people" as opposed to any "person" along the way – the intellectual community most amenable to his position in all of history – are those he celebrates as "classical" minds, with Plato principal among them. Thus he will say that "it appears that neither the We of any particular group nor a unique I, but man as man, is the measure of truth and untruth, of the being or unbeing of all things." His "man as man" is ultimately the philosopher, who arrives on the Western scene in Greece, rescuing knowledge beyond art itself. Thus Plato transcends Homer. The "highest kind of human knowledge that existed prior to the emergence of philosophy or science was the arts. But art is superseded in intellectual evolution by philosophy." That was a point to intellect in the history of intellect, a point at which intellect could make "prephilosophical distinction" between "artificial or man-made things and things that are not man-made." It is a distinction which thus "originally guided the quest for the first things." In recognizing this distinction, philosophy rises out of a recognition of "nature" as independent. "Nature was discovered when man embarked on the quest for the first things in the light of the fundamental distinctions between hearsay and seeing with one's own eyes, on the one hand, and between things made by man and things not made by man, on the other." Thus, both art and history are species of hearsay about nature, while science and philosophy are species of "seeing with one's own eyes."

It is this major movement of intellect toward "first things" that Strauss values over Voegelin's valuing of the moment to consciousness of a revelation in the desert, a moment out of which Voegelin builds his monumental work, *Order and*

History, whose first volume is called *Israel and Revelation*. Concerning revelation, Strauss remarks his opposition to any supposition of a reality leading to that concept. He maintains his independence as philosopher: "All arguments in favor of revelation seem to be valid only if belief in revelation is presupposed; and all arguments against revelation seem to be valid only if unbelief is presupposed." The latter for Strauss is the point of departure for philosophy, and at that fork of the intellectual road he chooses unbelief. Revelation as concept, then, becomes a sandtrap to philosophy, in his view. Strauss struggles by intellectual intent to maintain an independence through unbelief in revelation, a position freed of either belief or unbelief it is supposed. But a skepticism as allowing a freedom of objectivity leads to a struggle within circumstance to intellect which can only complicate his recognition of some necessity for "value judgments." For if one take the position of social science in his day (the post-World War II period) "we would not be permitted to speak of cruelty" in relation to our analysis of the phenomena of the Nazi concentration camps. Strauss, as philosopher, seems intent, then, on recovering himself to that ground of wonder in the moment of the recognition of nature as actual, in distinction from the hearsay of art or history. He would recover, perhaps, a state of intellectual nature in which it is neither concerned for an intellectual "We" nor for its own uniqueness as an "I." The concern is for "man as man," as the "measure of truth and untruth, of the being or unbeing of all things." What Voegelin objected to in Strauss's position is the impossibility of such a recovery of intellectual innocence, though he shared with Strauss a deep love of that ideal classical mind which Strauss would define by these restrictions.

Strauss's "natural" allies such as Voegelin and the more orthodox Christian philosophers of natural rights based in classical natural law may find in Strauss's version of it an aloofness, a detachment suggesting a skeptical closing of intellect against the possible and probable as those terms may be valid to classical natural law theory. For the Christian, of course, the acceptance of revelation as actual historical event, specifically that revelation of the Incarnation, will set aside both the possible and probable from the actuality of natural law and natural rights. Strauss's philosophy proves but another species of angelism. In accepting revelation, the Christian philosopher as proponent of natural law sees a necessity to philosophy that it be founded deeper than an attempt to recover an intellectual innocence through a deliberate – a willed – skepticism. That is the position taken by John Paul II in his *The Splendor of Truth*. These allies against Modernist deconstruction of reality nevertheless share in a desire to rescue the openness of the classical mind to the devotions possible to the truth of things, through at least an acknowledgment of the possible or probable. What one finds himself uneasy about in Strauss as ally is a hidden dogma held tenaciously, a faith denying faith, whereby he insists upon a libertarian divorce of intellect in the interest of its philosophical actions purified of commitment. For Strauss, commitment seems entrapment. It is thus that, in his devotions to Plato, for instance, his is a devotion from a skeptical position more that of the classical Stoic than the classical Platonist such as Voegelin. Plato's own entrapment of desire by truth itself becomes a case history in the rescue of the true philosopher. It is a history unresolved by Plato, foundering particularly in the dilemma of the One and the Many, though the ideal in Plato's intentionalities is always the truth of things.

This is the uneasy center of skepticism in Strauss's thought with which Eric Voegelin found himself most uncomfortable, though he attempts with a charity of intellect (irritating at last to Strauss) to persuade Strauss that faith, rather than being inimical to philosophy, is the moment in intellectual act out of which intellect is enabled to any philosophical act. It is a consent to *givenness* for Voegelin, a consent which Strauss rejects, rather haughtily, breaking off their correspondence. Voegelin, finding philosophy dependent upon givenness, seeks a resolution to the suspension of the soul in the

Platonic *metaxy* – the *In-between* experienced by consciousness and resolving the tensional poles to thought: the immanent and the transcendent. At the very end, he attempts to draw his monumental work, *Order and History*, to conclusion with Volume Five: *In Search of Order*, still on the way, still knowing – as did Plato's Socrates – that where one stands to see is within the seeing itself and therefore a complication to finite intellect.

That is a problem implicit in his final work, published as "*Quod Deus Dicitur,*" "What May be Said of God," published by the *Journal of the American Academy of Religion,* December 1985, soon after his death, in an unfinished state but with notations by his friend and assistant Paul Caringella of his intended end. The title itself is from St. Thomas, and the intended end was to be a consideration of Thomas's Question XIII of the *Summa,* the twelve articles on "The Names of God" as that problem may be addressed from where one stands to see. It is still Voegelin on the way toward the possibility of vision to intellect in a fulfillment of revelation, the reality of revelation itself never abandoned by him. One of the names of God, as Thomas himself insists along his own way, is Beauty, to which concern we shall presently return from where we ourselves now stand.

The orthodox defender of "natural right" or "natural law" may see in Strauss himself a species of angelism with ironic dimensions. For Strauss charges Hegel with having presumed his moment of history the ultimate moment. Strauss remarks that we "cannot see the historical character of 'all' thought . . . without transcending history, without grasping something trans-historical." But he would occupy that trans-historical position as philosopher by superseding the "prephilosophical distinction" between "artificial or man-made things and things that are not man-made." Only by that supersession may intellect address "first things," the necessity to a position flubbed by Hegel as philosopher. The angelistic position Strauss would occupy, then, is as intellectual philosopher, not a "We" nor an "I," but as "man as man," thus enabled to the "measure of truth and untruth, of being or unbeing of all things." But in the logic of that position, we must accept Strauss himself as *the* "man as man," he assuming authority by skeptical detachment from history and nature. And so this is the uneasy center to Strauss's thought with which Eric Voegelin found himself necessarily opposed, since it rejects any givenness, even of "man as man."

We have dwelt on this encounter of distinguished intellects, Strauss and Voegelin, because they so well represent the dilemma to a recovery of a traditional perspective upon the nature of man to what is now often called ambiguously a conservative position. But if we seem most conspicuously besieged in our moment by reductionist accounts of our nature as freed from the mystery of givenness by the magic of science, that strategy proves a most ancient one, when we explore it: the seeming necessity to freedom in a pretense to autonomy, the pretense to self-creation. Always that necessity, which in our day appears disturbingly effective as evidenced by gnostic process yielding the magic of technology. Through that technology the particularities of nature are declared measurable accidents in an absolute sense and therefore independent of that philosophical concept of being as a *given*. They are justifiably manipulated to conform to the moment's desire, as if what has been set aside by magic is the Cause of creation in the multitude of particularly existing things. The concept *God* is taken as intellect's own creation, to be transformed to the convenience of manipulation into a concept of the self as idol to be worshipped. That was T. S. Eliot's recognition, sung by his Chorus in *The Rock:* "men both deny gods and worship gods, professing first Reason, / And then Money, and Power, and what they call Life or Race, or Dialectic."

But sore oppressed by this Modernist inclination, it proves yet an oppression most ancient, implicit in the grace of our givenness to intellect called free will. Hence we have said it as ancient as the Garden of Eden – an inclination waxing and waning in the long history of intellect, moving under the aggressive banner *non servium*. At the risk of an excessive judgment, it seems in our moment a position almost triumphant over the truth of things. The victories of autonomous intellect in its rejections of the mystery of givenness seems almost universal (to adapt a Kantian term to the concern). And so at the lag-end of our millennium there appears a much-talked-of conclusion – the Hegelian end of intellectual history, trumpeted especially among intellectuals in strategic positions within the social and political and educational orders of making at our moment. The classical resistance to this perennial invasion of reality has bequeathed us those "classical" virtues, the shared cardinal virtues: *prudence, justice, fortitude, temperance*. (We well name them here, since they seem so far removed from us at this juncture of millennia.) To those traditionally classical virtues, necessary to the order of person and community, the theological virtues strengthen reason, the virtues descended through revelation and crucially supportive against the temptation not to serve: *faith, hope, charity*. This is a context of an inherited wisdom allowing an accommodation of Classical and Christian virtues through the devotions of the philosopher. For, as Eric Voegelin reminds us, it is the philosopher who makes his way intellectually because of his love of being, out of which fundament to existential reality, intellect has discovered its proper deportment as itself most mysteriously given. It is the philosopher who reminds us of the intellectual virtues necessary to that accommodation: the intellectual virtues of *knowl edge, understanding, wisdom* – to name them in an ascendant order toward intellectual perfection of *homo viator* in his limited givenness.

Through those virtues in consort, made resonant in intellect and thereby waking in it a desire for the good, intellect pursues the truth of things with that prudential humility which evidences at least a rudimentary accommodation of the Classical and Christian virtues. It is within that resonant intellectual arena, then, that St. Thomas can speak confidently of the artist's responsibility to the beautiful, arguing the artist as artist to be always concerned for the good of the thing he makes. (The parallel of this responsibility in the philosopher is for the truth of things.) Thomas, in rejecting as the artist's responsibility moral rectitude as art's end, would have us avoid seemingly practiced uses of art in a pursuit which will grow into self-righteousness in the artist (and note how self-righteous those artists among us in this moment who defend art's freedom to commit pornography). Thomas affirms as well the philosopher's responsibility to be governed by the truth of things in themselves, and it is as philosopher that he explores art as a "science" to intellect whereby *reason makes.*

That Leo Strauss could not at last accommodate himself to faith, hope, and charity as desirable to his intent to order the mystery of his own limited existence as intellect must have been a great sadness to Eric Voegelin. But beyond that sadness, Voegelin continues his own pursuit of a reconciliation. It seems significant, then, that in his end Voegelin attempts a rational engagement of modern man's dislocation from givenness by turning to Thomistic realism as a point of departure. (On the day before his eighty-fourth birthday, on January 2, 1985, Voegelin began dictating to Paul Caringella his "Quod Deus dicitur," that phrase from Thomas's *Summa Theologiae,* I, Q 13, his twelve articles on "The Names of God," revising the pages three days before he died on January 19th.) This much said, we may ourselves turn once more to our concern for the nature of beauty, to that language spoken to intellect out of things in themselves in respect to due proportion governed by essence.

That is a language summoning intellect to an accommodation of man's will to the mystery of givenness, corrective of that old temptation to its own autonomy as the only absolute. For here lies possible an accommodation of freedom to limited givenness – from the Christian philosopher's perspective. One is to be made perfect in *freedom* through *service* to the Cause of things in the actions of stewardship. (In one of the names of God, in a collect from the Anglo-Catholic *Prayer*

Book, he is that reality bursting names as inadequate, "whose *service* is *perfect freedom.*") We shall begin, then, by noticing among the names of God for St. Thomas, in that portion of the *Summa* which Voegelin begins to examine in his final attempt to reconcile intellectual order to intellectual ambiguities derived from nature and history, a name we must accommodate in freedom: Beauty.

Beauty:
That Which When Seen Pleases

i

Very early in the *Summa Theologiae*, St. Thomas engages the relation of the good to the beautiful. He counters an initial objection to the proposition of his Article Four (I, Q 5) that "goodness has the aspect of a final cause." The objection is that goodness is coequal to other causes, "For, as Dionysius says (*Div. Nom* iv) *Goodness is praised as beauty*. Therefore goodness has the aspect of a formal [not final] cause." In his counter to this objection, Thomas first addresses that effect upon intellect called *beauty*, and with a care to emphasize a difference between *effect* of and the *essential nature* of that which actively effects, in this instance *beauty*:

> Beauty and goodness in a thing are identical fundamentally; for they are based upon the same thing, namely, the form [of the existing "thing"]; and consequently goodness is praised as beauty. But they differ logically, for goodness properly relates to the appetite (goodness being what all things desire); and therefore it has the aspect of an end (the appetite being a kind of movement towards a thing). On the other hand, beauty relates to the cognitive faculty; for beautiful things are those which please when seen [*id quod visum placit*].

Here, *seen* carries a meaning deeper than the eye's seeing, as *appetite* carries a meaning deeper than sensual desire. One might put it thus: through the body, a thing is experienced sensually, beheld by the senses, but in the event of this experience of a thing that thing comes to be held in intellect as truth. Thus held in intellect, thus understood as *truth* corresponding to an essential reality of the thing beheld, the thing is also understood as beautiful by virtue of certain characteristics essential to the reality of that thing. Beauty thus is an effect attendant upon our seeing, knowing, understanding of the thing in itself by truth held in intellect. Truth is exemplar of the specific thing held in intellect, so to speak. Similarly, the term *appetite* ("goodness properly relates to the appetite") relates to a desire in intellect for a perfection, its beholding of the thing by its truth, according to the thing's essential nature as a created, extrinsic thing independent by its nature of the exemplar truth which is held in intellect. This independent nature of the thing according to its existing as *this* thing is a reality shared by things through being, though things are distinct from each other according to their several essential natures. To each by its created nature there is given a "kind of movement" implicit in the nature of each thing, an inclination in it toward the perfection of its own essential limits in being. That is a movement toward the good of itself as *this* thing. This is the reality of a thing whereby, in speaking of it logically, we say that it *is*.

Herein lies a complex of conceptions of the relation of the good and the true and the beautiful, which are not interchangeable terms insofar as our understanding orients intellect toward logical articulation – the necessity to finite discursive intellect in its quest for an accord with the orders of created beings. It is a complex involving subtle distinctions too easily obscured by our necessary discursiveness. Such distinctions may be obscured to us through (for instance) the elevation of aesthetics to a dominance in pursuit of order, as if order itself were effected by beauty as order's agent. *Homo viator* as poet may find himself disoriented from reality by such an inclination to beauty and thus tempted to affirm beauty as equal to or superior to goodness in the order of his intellectual deferences to complex reality. In abandoning necessary distinctions between the beautiful and the good, an artist (or his critic) may consequently too easily incline to a confusion of himself with God as *creator* insofar as he sees himself as the *creator* of beauty in the thing he would make (or, in the instance of the critic, the thing he would judge). It is a concern St. Thomas repeatedly engages in much of his works, this sorting of concepts accumulated from truths held in intellect out of experiences of things. For in that sorting of experience by reason, in pursuit of understanding, he would guard against an impetus of desire to distort complex reality of the thing as it must be properly held in the understanding. Either through impatience or carelessness of reason, but especially through an intent to power in elevating intellect over things as if it were the cause of things, desire may be willfully dislocated from the proper, proportionate end.

In the *Summa Contra Gentiles*, Thomas holds this steady concern, especially in relation to the Son as the Word. The distinction between creating and making is at issue, lest that ancient fall from being occasioned by a desire to be "as the gods" should dominate intellect. Thus in Book Four: Salvation, Chapter 11, he engages as its topic the question "How Generation Is to Be Understood in Divinity, and What Is Said of the Son of God in Scriptures." Of particular concern to Thomas here is the distinction between and the relation of the Word to the artist's word, and he introduces the opening passage of the Gospel of St. John on the topic. We see in the following quotation his concern for the word as engaged by the artist in his making as a foreshadowing to finite intellect of its proper response to existing as person, to its understanding of precedent mystery: man created in the *image* of God.

> [14] [T]he word interiorly conceived is a kind of account and likeness of the thing understood. . . . [E]ssentially an *exemplar* . . . an image if it is related to that whose like-

ness it is as to a principle. . . . [S]ince the likeness of the
artifact existing in the mind of the artist is the principle
of the operation which constitutes the artifact, the likeness is related to the artifact as an exemplar to that exem-
plified; but the likeness of a natural thing conceived in
our intellect is related to the thing whose likeness it is as
to its *beginning* from the senses which are changed by
natural things.

[15] Now, there is a difference between intellect and
sense, for sense grasps a thing in its exterior accidents,
which are color, taste, quantity and other of this kind, but
intellect enters into what is interior to the thing. And,
since every knowledge is perfected by the likeness
between the knower and the known, there must be in the
sense a likeness of the thing in its sensible accidents, but
in the intellect there must be a likeness of the thing
understood in its essence. Therefore the word conceived
in the intellect is the image or exemplar of the substance
of the thing understood. [The likeness in intellect of the
thing understood is called *the truth of the thing*, an *exemplar*
of essence.]

This argument would distinguish the role of our senses in
sensible actions, as opposed to the role of intellect as it knows
intuitively the "natural thing" according to its essence by
entering "into what is interior to the thing." And from the distinction we might gain a purchase of understanding of the
distortion occurring when we separate these complementary
deportments as if each were independent in our experiences
of things. Pornography, let us suggest, requires this separation. That is, pornography intends a violation of the thing by
reducing it to a merely sensual object. Indeed, the sins of
incontinence (lust, gluttony, avarice) require precisely this
separation of modes, whereby things existing in themselves
are in some wise violated as discretely existing things, to the
fundamental destruction (as Dante dramatizes the point in
early Hell) of the violator.

It is in this antipathy between incontinent violation and a deportment of piety toward created things as good that one may best distinguish the pornography which pretends to be art from true art. We have explored Tolstoy's failure to make this distinction. Out of this failure he becomes increasingly a puritan spiritualist, rejecting the good of creation itself. And so burdened by his own sense that as artist he is in some respect possessed by evil, or so it seems to him to be so, on those occasions of his writing good stories in spite of his rejections of the word because confounded by creation. Hence Tolstoy attempts a rescue of art by declaring its only legitimacy its primary service in obligation to moral perfection. But for Tolstoy, this means a moral action at last rejecting things in themselves leaving him confused in a contradiction. St. Thomas to the contrary, as we have emphasized, insists that art as an intellectual virtue bears as the artist's principle obligation, not moral perfection of an audience, but the artist's responsibility to the good of the thing he makes.

In the passage from the *Summa Theologiae* (I, Q 5, Art 4) following his definition of *beauty* as that which pleases when the thing is *truly* seen, he continues, having remarked the effect of beauty on human sensibilities. His concern becomes to define the essential characteristics of *beauty*:

> Hence beauty consists in due proportion; for the senses delight in things duly proportioned, as in what is after their own kind – because even sense is a sort of reason, just as is every cognitive faculty. Now, since knowledge is by assimilation, and similarly relates to form, beauty properly belongs to the nature of formal cause.

Such is the relation of the formal to the final, a relation to which Thomas must return again and again along his way, and again and again this proves an engagement of a distinction of the good and the beautiful in respect to *formal* as opposed to *final* cause. Consequently, the distinctions are of importance to the person in respect to that person's final end as a perfection in respect to his created nature as intellectual soul incarnate.

The formal cause of beauty in the artist's made thing depends consequently upon the artist's making through reason, whereby his informing action effects the made thing's being as a made thing. In relation to that perfection it is beautiful, beauty being an effect of a "due proportion." Art, in this respect, is a science proper to intellectual action, made a science through reason in deference to the good of the thing through formal proportion in its being. Whatever uses are made of the artifact subsequently, in the interest of moral perfection or of dissolution, are separate concerns from the responsibility to stewardship of the thing made by the artist by his gift of making. When this relation between making and the uses of the made thing becomes distorted, the artist's responsibility as artist will become distorted as well. Thus "political" art (such as that with which Lenin becomes obsessed in its Marxist uses) or "religious" art (such as one may still find in some Sunday School tracts) are not art according to the intellectual virtue proper to the artist, as that virtue is understood by the Thomist.

It will not follow, of course, that an exercise of art as an intellectual virtue will in no wise affect either the artist or his audience in the moral dimension of his human nature. Nevertheless, when the concern is a due proportion proper to the thing made, in an accord with the truth of things in themselves, that very engagement out of truth as intellectually held is consequent to experience of things in themselves. And since truth so derived is in a relation to the essential nature of things experienced, the orientation of the artist, knowingly or otherwise, is in some degree in ultimate reference to the Creator of the things experienced.

Consider the relation of the made thing to its origins in created things, as that relation is touched by implication in Aristotle's distinctions between art and history in his *Poetics*. That intellectual action called the making of a history is to be distinguished from that action called art. History as a made thing requires a virtue of science, reason in making, governed by the actual which is known as precedently actual – however tempting it becomes to convert history into fiction. That is a responsibility of the "historian" whether he be Thucydides writing *The History of the Peloponnesian War* or the historian of nature itself such as the genetic scientist in his laboratory. The artist as scientist – employing reason in making – is rather concerned for the *possible* or *probable*. But those concepts depend as well upon the actual. In this aspect of art distinguished from social or natural history, St. Thomas reminds us that the drama of art lies in an imitation, not of nature per se, but of the *action* of nature as reasonably understood. It is an understanding out of experience (which need not of course be actual – one need not have murdered to make a *MacBeth* or *Othello*). The concern for the action perceived in relation to the actual recovers for the artist the arena proper to drama as that of the possible or probable.

It is in recognition of this relation of intellectual science in response to the truth of things that leads Flannery O'Connor (out of her readings of St. Thomas) to comment on that attempted amalgamation of empirical history and art which yields those literary categories of "Realism" and "Naturalism." For, as she says in *Mystery and Manners*, if "a writer is any good, what he makes will have its source in a realm much larger than that which his conscious mind can encompass and will always be a greater surprise to him than it can ever be to his reader." And on another occasion, with specific reference to the Modernist spirit of the age, if the fiction writer, "in tune with this spirit," believes "that actions are predetermined by psychic make-up or the economic situation or some other determinable factor, then he will be concerned above all with an accurate reproduction of the things that most immediately concern man, with the natural forces that he feels control his destiny." If true to the good of the thing he makes in its dependence upon the actual, he "may produce a great tragic naturalism," since thereby he "may transcend the limitations of his narrow vision."

It is a point of extended concern in the *Summa*, I, Q 39, Art 8. Here in setting out, Thomas reminds us of a most central principle, which implies a refutation of both Manichean and various gnostic manipulations of formal and final causes and ends such as we have observed Lenin deploying to his political ends by dislocating the nature of art to effect those ends.

> Our intellect, which is led to the knowledge of God from creatures, must consider God according to the *mode* derived from creatures. In considering any *creature* four points present themselves to us *in due order*. Firstly, the thing itself taken absolutely is considered as a being. Secondly, it is considered as one. Thirdly, its intrinsic power of operation and causality is considered. The fourth point of consideration embraces its relation to its effects. Hence this fourfold consideration comes to our mind in reference to God.

The emphasis in the quoted passage is my own. For of concern to Thomas is the *limit* to human knowing consequent upon the person's nature as created thing and the consequent necessity to intellect therefore of ordering considerations of reality through reason. Our "mode" of knowing is intellectually engaged through creatures created. And the first engagement of that mode in cognitive response to the created thing is through the senses, which Thomas has declared "a sort of reason" (I, Q 5, Art 4). In the person's movement toward a knowledge of God, then, the senses as cognitive means is a first movement of consciousness within the surrounding complex to intellect which we call creation. That first movement leads in a progress toward understanding – in the ordering of cognitive faculties to the person – to a limited knowing of God afforded by that principle of proportionality, a principle gradually understood by intellect. For we come to see proportion in the orders of creation in relation to the absolute perfection and cause of creation, God. It is in this movement of intellect that God is anticipated intuitively as Absolute Beauty because Absolute Good, an intuited knowing to be explored by rationally knowing.

In considering "in due order" the truth of *a* created thing experienced by intellect, intellect knows a thing as a *being*, as

a *one*, and as possessing therefore intrinsic "power of operation and causality" as consequent upon its being a created
one. The relationships engaged among these "points" of
knowing are thus to be considered in due order according to
our experience of things. Consideration in accord, in "due
order," leads toward a recognition called rationally knowing,
leading to an understanding partaking of both the rational
and intuitive modes of knowing. Understanding, a person
concludes that he has experienced a unique – because *created*
– thing. Such a moment of understanding may allow to intellect the moment of revelation. Recall, for instance, that
moment in which Dame Julian of Norwich sees in the hazel-
nut on her palm the mystery of all creation as Caused by
Love. In that visionary moment there is revealed to her the
continuous presence to every thing of that sustaining Love, a
Love which Thomas examines in its manifestations to reason
through his logic, under the rubrics of causality encountered
through proportionate analogy. Knowing, actively pursued
by intellect toward understanding, always borders upon that
grace called revelation, whereby any thing – as do all things
created – "comes to our mind in reference to God." Put yet
once more, knowledge inwardly digested by a right will to
know provides the intellectual an energy to its understanding, to the health of the journeying soul toward its own perfection. And here, "right will" intends to suggest a turning
through intellect out of the self in an action called love. It is
intellectual action moving the person toward the possible
border upon intellect called revelation, the effect of an act of
grace.

In this respect, we might say that by the artist's attention
to the good of the thing he makes, his attention partakes of
love, with the implicit temptation that it may prove inordi-
nate, as the myths of both Narcissus and Pigmaleon – not to
say the several dramas of Faustus – suggest. Further, in
another perspective upon his deportment, the artist's actions
of love in the interest of the good of the thing he makes may
prove a source of that popular suspicion of the artist as

always "aloof," as separated from community, a response which the artist himself on occasion exacerbates by a withdrawal in his devotion to his art. That became a Romantic elaboration of the image of the artist in the 19th century. But the devotion of love when ordinate in the artist, speaking his proper devotion to his own peculiar gifts, may also be a source of the popular inclination to see oneself as poet. What that inclination intuitively speaks, from our argument, is the necessity to the person as intellectual soul incarnate – whatever peculiar gifts he may be graced by – that he be devoted to the good of whatever it is his gift to make, whether as poet or gardener, physician or politician, bricklayer or architect. And this is, once more, to emphasize as the principal obligation to stewardship the perfection of the person's specifically given nature as intellectual soul incarnate.

In this article (I, Q 39, Art 8), Thomas reflects on his points by rational consideration of the "nature" of God. He does so with his own finite, and hence limited and ultimately inadequate, intellect. Those limits are reflected by the limits of intellect's own unique nature in relation to possible perfection. Those who see in Thomas – as many since him have seen – an arrogant presumption of his powers as an intellect have been able to do so only because they ignore a fundamental humility in him, a humility explicitly evident, for instance, in some of his hymns and prayers. But here in the *Summa* his concern is for the logical relation to the Son – that *"principle without a principle"* in the mystery of the Trinity – of man himself as maker, as an image of that Son. For the Son is "the express image of the Father," an act of Love as Revelation, in relation to which "expression" lie the gifts of limits to our personhood. Thus both *species* and *beauty* have their likeness in us as persons, as things, in the "property of the Son." That is one of the meanings of the Incarnation, through which a divine condescension restores a dignity to us as a *being*, a *oneness* as is true *proportionately* of each created thing. It is a potential to us as created, restored to us by hope through that incommensurate first sacrifice called the Incarnation, in

Whom the final sacrifice is in rescue of the being and oneness of each created person. That is the sacrifice revealed through the Crucifixion. The most central rescue in all creation is of man, in particular manifestation: *this* person as the image of God. And by that rescue it may recovered, as proximate always, our right will to a worldly sojourn in ordinate responsibility of stewardship to things.

But what is this effect of "beauty" experienced mystically in the revelation, and how does it relate to the effect of beauty as we experience beauty in any thing? Beauty, says Thomas, "includes three conditions, *integrity* or *perfection*, since those things which are impaired are by that very fact ugly; due *proportion* or *harmony*; and lastly, *brightness*, or *clarity*, whence things are called beautiful which have [for example] a bright color." These are conditions attendant upon the reality of a thing, consequent from its *being* and its *oneness* as created thing, and proportionately caused by a Love whereby it "lives and breathes and has its being" in that famous formulation by which created things are understood as sustained by the Comfort of Love to their existing, by the Holy Spirit. And, since the Son's property *is* as the "express Image of the Father," and because of the Son's intersection of creation in the Incarnation, it is in that "Image" that we discover most certainly the due proportion and harmony characteristic of beauty. "Hence we see that an image [as opposed to the Image of the Father] is said to be beautiful, if it perfectly represents even an ugly thing." For what is perceived as beauty, even in the ugly thing, is a relation of actuality of the thing to the potentiality of that thing as a grace to its given nature, the integrity of that thing lying in its possible perfection of the gifts of its essential being.

As for the "*brightness* and *clarity*, whence things are called beautiful," that is revealed to us in that property of the Son "as the Word, which is the light and splendor of the intellect," shared proportionately through that Word by the person in that he is a created intellect, but especially created in the image of God. It is this aspect (says Thomas) of our relation to

the Word to which Augustine alludes when he says of Christ
(in *De Trinitate*) that he is "As the perfect Word, not wanting
in anything, and so to speak, the art of the omnipotent God."
In that figuring in relation to man's art, we might say, it is the
Son as Image in relation to which we come to understand the
nature of image in intellect as mediating finite intellect to created things, and thence ultimately to the Cause of created
things. The artist, then, will reflect that Image to the world in
some degree of his action of making – assuming gifts to him
as artist and his prudent exercise of those particular gifts by
his making through *reason,* as Thomas will say. The artist so
oriented through the Word engages prospects of beauty to his
made thing. He thus effects an integrity or perfection, a proportion and brightness or clarity, in the thing he makes.

It will follow, then, that the poet's made "image" – his
imitation not of nature but of the actions of nature – will be in
degree beautiful. It will be so "if it perfectly represents even
an ugly thing." Here, "perfectly represents" is understood as
related to the peculiar gifts of the artist, for we do not understand the made thing is in itself beautiful because of an
absolute representation of a perfect thing independent of creation itself, for that is a contradiction in terms. It is nevertheless a contradiction obscure to the artist himself insofar as he
may mistake himself as creator rather than maker, presuming
himself and his word not simply analogous by correspondence to the Perfect Artist and his Word, whereby the human
artist and his word are equated proportionately to God and
his Word. The distortion of the reality of the artist himself
begins when he presumes himself the absolute cause of his
made thing. From that error the artist presumes himself an
Identity with, rather than image of, the Creator. How easily
out of such careless analogy may the poet reject God and
Word, to be replaced by the poet and his poem. That, we
recall, is the destructive dilemma to James Joyce's young
Stephen, who attempts to establish himself as artist, as
autonomous creator, through an absolute rejection of all save
his own intellect. He, young Stephen – and possibly Joyce to

a degree himself – tends to forget the limiting proportionality of the artist as a created being in his relation to God as Absolute Being. Stephen does so through the seduction of his intellect by his will to presume himself the first cause of beauty. He would pronounce the artist the absolute cause of beauty through some species of rejection whose fundamentalist rubric is *non servium*. To the contrary, Maritain speaks of the distinction properly governing the artist in his *Art and Scholasticism*: "God's love *causes* the beauty of what He loves, whereas our love *is caused by* the beauty of what we love" (my emphasis). A proper orientation of intellect to beauty is thus simply put. But how difficult to possess the principle of this differentiation as an operative vision to our making!

ii

In Book Two: Creation of the *Summa contra Gentiles*, Thomas engages a question of the unity of intellect, as he has done more extensively in his treatise against the Averroists. His Chapter 75 of the *Contra Gentiles* is labeled "Demonstrative Arguments for the Unity of the Possible Intellect." His argument, among its several concerns, is for the nature of art in two species of art as exercised by intellect within creation. It is the "active principle" in the "matter" of each of these two arts which here interests us, in our concern for the question of the perfection of the possible intellect through actions of art. Thomas observes that "there exists an art whose matter is an active principle tending to produce the effect of that art." He illustrates by naming the arts of medicine and of teaching, in contrast to the art of building. Medicine and teaching, Thomas says, are arts engaging the restorative or perfective *given* nature in the "matter" proper to the art. In medicine and teaching, the end is health and knowing, and the matter involved is for the one the body's health, for the other a fulfillment of intellect in knowing. These differ in respect to the matter involved if we contrast them to that of the art of building, in that "wood and stone do not have in them an active force tending to the construction of a house."

As for the intellect, it bears "an active principle conducive to knowledge," a principle to be engaged by the teacher. To know is a proper necessity to the perfection of intellect according to its given nature. And in respect to this proper necessity, the art of teaching (which does not exclude self-teaching), Thomas says that it is an art exercised "to imitate nature." We engage this point here to uncover a distinction to be made concerning the art of teaching, which requires a perfection of intellect through knowing as differing from that art required in a subsequent operation out of that knowing which we speak of as the art of the poet. (Here we shall use the poet as representative, though the argument applies as well to painters or musicians, or indeed to each of us as by nature a *maker*.) If, as Thomas says, "Art work presupposes work of nature," whatever the art (whether building or making poems), our distinction here is with a concern for a primary and a secondary aspect of art as peculiar to the poet. When to learn is primary, teaching is concerned with an "imitation of nature" in respect to the perfection of intellect, whereby we say that intellect comes to "know the truth of things" as they are in themselves, a knowing of a thing in correspondence to the essence of the thing. Thereby through understanding, intellect itself may receive perfection. In respect to this concern we say that intellect thus proves conducive to its own perfection through an inherent desire to know as the initial principle of its nature. Through the "active principle conducive to knowledge" – the desire to know – the potential intellect becomes actual. We do not, however, conclude from this initial principle that by desire it thus defines the final end of knowing. Rather, to desire to know is to be on the way toward the final end.

If we turn to this peculiar knowing agent, the poet as man on his way, and consider his desire as poet to bring into existence out of his knowing a poem, the "matter" he would perfect by form does not depend primarily through his "imitation of

nature," though it may be said to do so in a secondary manner. If we consider effects from the center of the agent in his
act of making, so to speak, we take a different perspective
upon the relation of primary and secondary effects of making.
For in the action of making, the poet's primary concern is for
the good of the thing he is making, a concern for the possible
perfection of the poem. There is by that concern a self-surren-
der as it were, setting aside for the poet his attention to his
own perfection as his primary end. A surrender of himself to
the good of the thing he would make is to act through a sacrificial love, though a sacrificial act of love incommensurate to
that of the Crucifixion, of course. Put in other terms, we may
say that the *poet* is a person making a poem, but the poem
once made, he is a person *one* of whose actions in journeying
as intellectual soul incarnate has been that making. All his
actions contribute, by effects most various, toward (or, in a
failure of action, away from) his perfection as person.

From this perspective we might consider whether it is
likely that, if in his act of making the poem the poet's primary
concern becomes for his own perfection, he will fail in some
degree in making perfect his poem, as he may also thereby
fail in some degree his own perfection as person – a perfection of his specific gifts of being, for which he is responsible.
It is a failure sometimes recorded in spectacle, as when the
poet's concern becomes for fame or acclaim and his making
turned to making instruments toward some aspect of a
worldly end as primary, affecting his devotion to the good of
the thing he makes. What is at issue, then, is a certain self-for-
getfulness (not an indifference to audience as may often be
charged against him) accomplished through actions moved
by love beyond a primary concern for the possible effects
upon the self. That is why the artist so committed may not be
content until he has perfected the back of his statue which
will never be seen by his audience – to speak figuratively.

Now this distinction between primary and secondary
effects of making a poem, seen from the poet's perspective in
his act of making, becomes important lest the poet mistake as

his primary operative principle an imitation of nature. Rather, Thomas argues, his operative principle, governing imaginative speculation in his making, is an imitation of the *action* of nature. Put another way, the *action* of nature he recognizes as differing from the actual effect through his speculative imagination. It is a recognition in relation to what Aristotle has called, as we have remarked, the *possible* or *probable* as distinct from the *actual* – the actual being the province of the science of history. It is in relation to this distinction that we may reflect further on Thomas's emphasis that the poet's primary focus of responsibility in making must be upon the good of the thing being made. This insistence distinguishes a prudential concern for right doing of the person as person from the art of making of a thing in this present moment. But this is to distinguish, not to disjoin, making and doing. Considered disjoined, they may appear irrelevant to each other – a disjoining all too easily accomplished by the poet insofar as he may lose his sense of responsibility to the good of the thing he makes.

That is a loss perhaps occurring when the poet's speculative imagination pursues the possible or probable beyond the bounds of nature's limit, the bounds of the actual, in which pursuit he must suppose himself creator and not maker. For the actual is the arena of dependence wherein the poet has his prudential responsibilities of becoming as an intellectual soul incarnate in relation to the gifts implicit in creation itself – his being as person in his actual and potential limits. The poet, given imaginative enthusiasm prompted by his recognitions of the possible or probable in responses to the actual, may loosen imaginative ties to reality – to the actual – and incline to fanciful liberations from the actual – in willful violations not only of the actual but of the possible or probable he has recognized through recognition of the actions of nature. Henry James is "Realist," in a famous figure through which by intention he would set himself apart from the "Romantic." The Romantic he speaks of is inclined to art as a balloon unanchored. The Realist instead tethers the made thing in the actual. If the "Romantic" loosen that anchor in reality, his made thing becomes victim to the winds of fancy as it were.

The poet may especially be tempted to free his imaginative speculations in his making to the whims of fancy, and the more so if he has also been tempted to believe himself as poet to be creator rather than maker. That became a troubling concern to Coleridge as "Romantic," this troubling concern for the relation of fancy to imagination when will elevates itself as autonomous. And it is in this respect that we have what we may see as the "last of the Romantics" in James Joyce's young artist Stephen, who would transcend existential reality, freed of that reality by his fanciful actions as poet. And we might recall as well that very poignant question Joyce will put to himself near the end of his life, wondering if he himself has not been rather a poet of the fancy than of the imagination. The poignancy reflects his fear of having failed as artist through his own willfulness, a temptation one of whose sources is Schiller.

If Thomas is insistent that the poet's responsibility as artist is to the good of the thing he is making, that responsibility implies a recognition of an inescapable dependence upon the created in the act of making. That will be a steady reminder to the poet that he makes with the given. It is in this implication we suggest that one finds a relevance of a secondary effect upon the poet consequent upon his making, namely a perfection (by degree) of his own intellect through prudential humility. Considered in relation to a present action of making, we may remark this a secondary effect in a complex of action in the poet on his way as person. From within that present action, if the secondary effect of making upon his own becoming arrests him as a primary concern, he may be led to suppose art salvific in itself and thus be tempted to make his art an idol through which he is tempted to worship his own power to perfect his made thing. Thomas will speak emphatically to this point, saying that the poet exercises by his art of making "a right reason" toward the good "of things made." That is a use of reason differing from reason's use in respect to prudence, whereby a right reason is directed to "things to be done" in accordance to the responsibility of the doer to his own perfection. In this respect, prudence may be said to remove obstacles to that grace sustaining the prudent person in his becoming. And in this respect, the "prudent" necessity to the poet is his devotion beyond any primary concern for himself, through a surrender of his gifts to the good of the thing he is making – gifts of making peculiar to him as *this* specific person.

Prudence requires the "moral virtues" to be primary, in order to rectify the appetite. "On the other hand the good of things made by art [such as the poet's poem] does not presuppose rectitude of the appetite," Thomas says. For this art of the poet "confers the mere aptness for good work." This perspective upon making, then, speaks to a virtue proper to the poet as maker differing from that of prudence to that same maker in respect to his personhood. It is a difference of attention to a present responsibility, to a present intellectual act of making. For the virtue of prudence confers both an aptness for a good work and confers use as well, Thomas says, in being concerned for the rectitude of appetite. Thus "the good of things made by art is not the good of man's appetite but the good of the things themselves," the poem in our designation (*Summa Theologiae*, Question 55, "Of the Virtues, As to Their Essence," Article 4). Thus the proposition of the preceding Third Article is explored, which affirms that "Art is nothing else but the right reason about certain works to be made."

And so with respect to this distinction between the virtues of prudence and of art, we should observe that those virtues are not exclusive of each other in the intellect of man as he makes a thing, a poem. In a larger perspective of prudential concern for salvation, the concern of Thomas's Book Four of *Summa Contra Gentiles*, it is the virtue of prudence which is seen as ultimately ascendant through right reason, and properly so.

For it is through prudence that the poet journeys toward his proper end, his making of things along his way from that dimension of concern secondary to this final end. Nevertheless, his peculiar gift as poet requires his steward-ship of that gift. What concerns us, then, is that primary prin-ciple to the making of a poem in this present moment of mak-ing, in respect to the action of intellect as it makes this poem. For it is by this concern that beauty rises to perception from the well-made thing. In this perspective, the poet's concern must be for the good of the thing he makes, not a concern for his own self-rescue nor for a rectitude of appetite in others. One might put as governing rubric: Devote the gift of making, peculiar to the person as artist, to the good of the thing he is making, and rectitude of appetite will take care of itself as a consequence of his ordinate stewardship – insofar, that is, as the perceivers of the beauty of the made thing themselves respond by right will.

To fail in this distinction between primary and secondary concerns in the midst of the act of making, if one is making a poem, is likely to reduce the poem from art to tract. That is a point to reiterate as necessary. And we well remember that "Sunday School tracts" are not the only species of art as tract. Joyce's Stephen becomes bent upon tract at the expense of his gift as poet by denying and rejecting reality. The poet, in rela-tion to his various dependencies as person upon the several arts proper to the nature of his intellect itself, is required to a dependency in a proper orientation within the nature of cre-ated things. The artist, this is to say, cannot reject the orders of being. Intellect in its very givenness is responsible as steward to the orders of being. Thereby the poet must recognize the very limits of his responsibility as maker predicated to him as intellectual creature by the orders of being. And by that recog-nition he reaches an accommodation to givenness signified by our term for his deportment: prudential humility. It is through the gift to intellect itself, a gift of participation by intellect in Divine Providence called the gift of "natural law," that he discovers the limits of his responsibility upon which depend (if he be poet) his recognitions of the possible or probable. Thus he may understand the actions of nature prudentially as sustained in nature in relation to intellect itself. Creation thus becomes the initial mediator to intellect of that sustaining Love, the Creator of nature. And that is why the poet must, for the good of the thing he makes, understand that his is not the gift of art to be perfected by virtue of imitating nature *actual* but is rather to be governed as act to his making by speculative dependences upon the *actions* of nature.

As for man, created in the image of God and so echoing his Cause in the world of nature, the particular essence of that echoing is out of his peculiar gift as maker. He echoes his Cause, to speak figuratively, in relation to his free will, in a proportionate fulfillment of his own specified being as *this* person. St. Thomas is acutely aware always of this similarity between incommensurate natures – that between the ineffable Creator and his created surrogate to a stewardship of the good, man. By analogy, and always careful of proportionality between man as image and God as Cause, St. Thomas prepares to maintain "That Things Which God Does Apart from the Order of Nature Are Not Contrary to Nature," a defense of God's prerogative of miracle as exempted from logical contradiction. Thomas says (in Chapter 100 of Book Three: Providence in the *Contra Gentiles*): "[A]ll creatures are related to God as art products are to an artist. . . . Consequently, the whole of nature is like an artifact of the divine artistic mind. But it is not contrary to the essential nature of an artist if he should work in a different way on his product, even after he has given it its first form. Neither, then, is it against nature if God does something to natural things in a different way from that to which the course of nature is accustomed" – that is, according to its created nature. Here, perhaps, we touch upon the crux wherein the poet may so easily mistake himself as creator rather than maker, the danger to him we have emphasized.

For an imaginative "revision" of his made thing's "first form," a changing of perspective by the maker, in respect to the possible or probable "matter" to his made thing, may occasion in him an exhilaration out of a revision of the old envisioned work, tempting a presumption of his own absoluteness.

In wonder and awe before his own discovery of good to the thing he would make perfect through form as imaginatively supplied (out of the possible or probable derived from the action of created things) his own act of making may well seem to partake of the miraculous. For even as we may in awe wonder why *something* rather than *nothing* exists, in relation to existential reality, the poet may wonder additionally *why this beautiful thing I am making comes to be when it was not.* The work partakes of the miraculous, though in a dependence upon the truly miraculous – the world of created things – so that the proportionate relation of maker to Creator may become obscure to the poet in the excited moment of his making. As a parallel to what Thomas speaks of as that "most excellent way" in which man as intellectual soul incarnate "partakes of a share of providence, being provident both for itself and for others," the poet so provident of the good of the thing he makes may easily lose sight of his created "natural inclination to [his] proper act" as maker.

Thomas is speaking, we recall, of a participation in the eternal law by virtue of the maker's being a "rational creature," a rational participation we call "natural law" (*Summa Theologiae*, I-II, q 91, a. 2). For man as maker, and in our instance the poet, it is through this participation in divine providence that he is allowed some purchase of understanding out of his experiences of the actual. If he is a poet, that understanding yields to the uses of his imagination engaging the possible or probable, allowing his *forming* that possible or probable in an imitation of the *action* of nature. (Hence the imitation is not of *nature actual*, as Thomas argues the distinction.) Such is the complex of that visionary moment to Dante, recorded as he concludes his *La Vita Nuova:* following his last sonnet, there occurred to him "a miraculous vision . . . in which I beheld things which made me determined never to speak of that blessed lady [Beatrice] until I could write worthily of her." That is the miraculous vision out of which will grow *The Divine Comedy,* yielding for him as person a "New Life" beyond that old version of life through which he had *informed* the "sonnets." In that old version there hovers implicitly a confidence in the poet as if he were creator rather than maker.

It is out of this conversion as poet, through the miraculous vision granted through his imaginative power, that Dante's recovery begins in the dark wood of the old vision in which he is graced by beholding things with eyes opening anew. What we may speculate, in relation to the metaphysical vision of man as intellectual soul incarnate as adumbrated by St. Thomas, is that Dante now is enabled to recognize and accept his powers of making. That wondrous thing to be made is neither *ex nihilo* nor instantaneous in respect to reason's informing that vision. Ahead is a labor to make resonant the possible or probable as specifically related to the actualities of his own created nature, biding in his own specific nature. His is to be a long labor of journeying, in which transit of creation as *homo viator* he must recover the several virtues proper to him as both poet and person, the virtues proper to both intellectual action and to the moral perfection toward which he becomes steward in response to his own givenness. Thus begins the agony of spirit to be undertaken in the making of *The Divine Comedy,* an agony actual to Dante not simply as maker but as person in transit to his proper end as person. And so there lies open to him a prospect for an accommodation of his nature to its given limits through the virtues of prudence and the virtues of art. As he must know, and as we all may well come to know, that accommodation is possible to the understanding only within the enlarging and including mystery of God's providence, in which alone the powers of the miraculous abide. It is in that context to miracle that he at last makes that poem which we call "divine."

And so the importance of humility in recognizing the created limits of the poet. In the *Contra Gentiles*, Book Three: Providence, Thomas prepares a distinction such as that more directly engaged in the *Summa Theologiae* in respect to the relation of the virtues of prudence to the virtues of art. "Art work presupposes work of nature," but the "artistic form that is produced in matter proceeds from the form that is in the mind of the artist." In orienting this art form by imaginatively engaging the possible or probable, in an imitation of the action of nature, Thomas advises the artist that "a lower type of art receives its principles from a higher one." Thus as God, the Absolute Artist, stands in relation to created things, the artist stands to his made thing, but only in respect to an incommensurate *proportionality* between the Absolute Artist God and the finite artist, the poet. That is why we say that the poet's made thing *depends from* nature as nature depends from its Creator. It is why we say as well that by making we share proportionately in a stewardship of an already limited antecedent *givenness*.

At the end of his life, Thomas returns to this concern in his sermons on the Apostles' Creed. He observes that the person as maker is a maker of the particular, for he is "not able to draw . . . form without material determined and presupposed," being "limited to the form alone, and therefore he can be the cause only of this form" which emerges in his made thing. "God, however, is the universal cause of all things, and God creates not only the form but also the matter." In this perspective the person is prevented just claim to a credit for his own "informed being," though by his presumption of intellect as autonomous he may suppose otherwise. As person he is responsible for a fulfillment of the "informing" gifts as this specifically created being designated as *this intellectual soul incarnate*. The poet's depending in being in his given nature is consequent upon his *being this* specific created nature. It is in the light of this truth of his givenness that we derive the crucial distinction of terms: the poet *makes*; God *creates* and has no property of dependence as does his image. As a tangent to this distinction therefore we gain some purchase upon the mystery involved in our saying that man is created in the image of God. It is a relation of proportionality incommensurate, insofar as man exists as a given. Even in the most wondrous imaginative actions of his making he cannot dream through them that he has bridged the disproportion. The separation in this disproportionality yields only to that incommensurate love, which touches him in his most inward givenness, a love which in Christian terms is called the Incarnation. Man cannot save himself by making, by his art.

As image of the Creator, then, man is a maker dependent in his actions upon a presupposition counter to the properties properly attributed to a creator. Preceding any actions of making is created nature, including that of the maker himself. Thomas, we saw,• puts the point insistently in his *Contra Gentiles*, Book Three: Providence: "Art work presupposes work of nature." One further point of importance, in respect to the distinction between that virtue in man called prudence, in relation to that virtue in him of art as enabling gift to his making. If the poet in his primary responsibility as maker is charged with the good of the thing he makes, and if he as poet makes imaginatively a *possible* or *probable* thing in imitation of the action of nature, in this respect those actions of nature serve in yielding imaginatively a form as if primary matter to his imaginative form. That is, such "actions" of nature serve art as its "matter," to which the poet supplies his imagined form as commensurate – through a reason oriented to the realities of his dependencies. Or so it may well appear to that maker when, the made thing at last before him, he responds with awe: here is a *new* thing under the sun. Wonder, following awe, may easily therefore confuse the maker in such response, as if limited form were an absolute action – as if by the making givenness itself were superseded. The maker will thereby have forgotten himself as providentially dependent as image of God and with an additional dependence within the complex realities of creation itself.

Now here our further point is well reiterated, concerning that effect upon the poet as person, a consequence to his making. It was a concern we initially set aside as secondary to the poet's concern in his present act of making which requires the good of the thing a-making as his primary devotion in the moment of making. Through the art of making, the maker is proved – is tested and perfected according to his precedent gifts essential in his nature as *this* person that lie in him potentially. He is proved and improved, so to speak, according to his existential free nature as *this* person existing in the image of God and acting out of that givenness. Thus, from his own perspective as maker there accrue secondary effects to his making – his own becoming. But though secondary in the present event of his making as he concentrates on the good of the thing in hand (i.e., in a present intentionality to make *this* thing imaginatively engaged), it is in the light of eternity hardly secondary. It has to do ultimately with his salvation. (This is the theme of Thomas's final Book of the *Contra Gentiles*, following his Book Three: Providence, a book concerned with man's final end, his salvation.) In Book Three: Providence, Thomas observes that "from the action of an instrument there is produced in the artifact a likeness of the form of the mind of the artist." It is a form mediated between artist and artifact by "the model in the mind of the maker of the thing to be made," which Thomas designates as the action of "art" (Book One: God). Our point here is that there is also a reciprocal effect of this action of making – an increased perfection, a becoming, of the making intellect when the thing he makes is good in itself. That is one of the implications implicit in Thomas's saying, in the *Summa Theologiae* (I, Question 39, Art 8), regarding beauty, that the made thing may radiate beauty, "if it perfectly represents even [a seemingly] ugly thing."

In this imitation of the possible or probable action of nature, then, there is effected a certain perfection of the maker's own intellect through the act of making virtuously pursued through reason. It is a perfection effected through his devotion in art to his special calling as this unique creature whose proper stewardship of his own gifts is this present making. We have concentrated upon the poet as maker, but should be aware as well that the argument implies making variously observed. For instance, the argument applies implicitly to the making of a table, or as St. Teresa observes even a keeping of pots and pans in a kitchen. He cannot in the exercise of this responsibility to his own nature at once and equally attend to the good of the thing he is making (poem or stew) and to the perfection of himself, as if the primary concern in his action in the moment of his making were his own perfection. He cannot, since he is not as intellect omniscient. (It would be otherwise were he truly Creator.) What is required, let us say, is a self-forgetting through a devotion to the good of the thing he makes, and that self-forgetting is an act of love. It is, as we suggested, a sacrificial act. That is one reason that the art of making a poem differs from the art of perfecting intellect through reflective knowing. If the poet were indeed equal to God, as he may sometimes suppose himself in respect to all the arts of Absolute Being (the arts properly absolute only in the Creator), his perfect and simple unity of being might indeed be that of an Absolute Perfection. That has been and is the dream of some poets, alas, who imagine themselves as independent of both nature and nature's God. That is the gist of Stephen Dedalus's *non servium* we observed along our way. For Thomas, the poet is rather a maker dependent as *image* of the Creator, as we have argued, who is further dependent as well upon those gifts always specific (limited) in created things. He is dependent as we say both *from* and *upon* given "nature," from which dependency he summons imaginatively the *actions* of nature to his making.

We are on the verge of a very old failing of man as artist here, if we recall the dislocation spoken of anciently as occurring in that old garden, the temptation whereby man would be not simply "like" God as image but "equal" to the "gods," knowing absolutely both good and evil. Out of that fall, proceeds the tangled relation of the good, the true, and the beautiful which ensnares intellect. The untangling of relations here is a long and arduous responsibility to intellect, whatever its special calling, as it struggles to recover an ordinate way. It is a way we each sojourn – proportionately according to our specific gifts as *this* person. And along that way we must be governed proportionately: in coming to know the proportionate place of any thing experienced within the orders of creation; in coming to know the principles implicit in intellect itself which are to be recovered – perfected according to their limit – through several arts proper to intellect. These are actions toward a perfection of *homo viator* as person in his simple unity, out of which those always eroding problems to intellect occur in its relating the good, the true, and the beautiful, which the person struggles to reconcile through his husbandry in making, the stewardship proper to man. It is *toward* a simple unity as *intellectual soul incarnate* that the person would move in his desire for that simple unity, in which unity all the virtues may at last dissolve through proportionality into a simple condition: a unity of openness toward that Absolute Unity through a responsive surrender of the person in sacrificial love. This is the direction in which the *person* moves in hope of Beatitude, whatever the particular calling of his stewardship along his way. For the poet, his journeying is toward Dante's vision of the multifoliate rose, however different his *con-figuration* of that ultimate Rose may be as revealed in the things he makes, things he leaves us in witness of his journey.

The effect of beauty he may himself have experienced through his making, though he will have come to understand perhaps that such local experience is not of beauty as an end in itself. Such experience but sustains him in his gifts, in anticipation of an encounter with ultimate Beauty, in which encounter perhaps *homo viator* becomes consumed in a perfection beyond all the labors of his journeying, whether as poet or whatever his local calling to stewardship in creation. Short of that anticipation, he always engages a local creation most fully only as person: all the wonders of diverse creation that touch him proximately on his journey in pursuit of the anticipated – that Love. Along that way, any created thing reveals itself as truth to him, speaking the mystery of the good and the beautiful as entangled in the challenges to his intellectual action. That is the revelation to Dame Julian of Norwich, holding the hazel-nut on her open palm and recognizing that it is sustained by Love so that it does not fall to nothingness despite its littleness. It is the recognition that leads the poet Flannery O'Connor as a "realist of distances" to say that "The longer you look at one object, the more of the world you see in it," so that "it's well to remember that the serious fiction writer always writes about the whole world, no matter how limited his particular scene. For him, the bomb that was dropped on Hiroshima affects life on the Oconee River [in middle Georgia], and there's not anything he can do about it."

Beauty then is the gift to intellect itself, mediated through created things whereby the person anticipates his ultimate end, stirring in him a desire whose object is beyond proximate ends and so keeps hope alive. Such is that complication to our journeying summarized by Maritain in saying that while "God's love causes the beauty of what he loves" in the multitudinous witness to a transcendent Love borne by things created, it is only at last through our answering love that we properly respond in opening a way to Love. It is through our opening love that we discover that "our love is caused by the beauty of what we love," a beauty most various, but speaking always that Absolute Beauty of Absolute Love: that which, "when seen," pleases beyond all our anticipations. That such is an ever-present truth along the way cries out to us continuously, as St. Augustine discovered when he listened to the things of creation in the music of their witness. For "With a mighty voice they [cry] out, 'He made us!'" Each thing singly sings by the beauty of its own nature which is to be loved: "I am not he, but he has made me!" That is the mystery of Love, spoken to us, says St. Augustine, by all the things that "stand around the doors of [our] flesh. . . ." The answer to the importunate question for St. Augustine is that things speak "their beauty." Beauty proportionately responded to justifies our love of "a certain light, a certain voice, a certain odor, a certain food, a certain embrace when I love my God." There is a serenity here which not many poets or philosophers can maintain, of course, since it is the effect we call happiness in the saint.

Afterword:
Thematic Notes

A) One of the themes implicit and overt along our way has been the relation of the poet as person to his actions as poet in making a thing reflecting reality more largely than as merely autobiography. How is he to disengage himself as an actual person from his attempt to dramatize with "due proportion" the possible or probable, in order that he may imaginatively catch art's reality as differing from nature's reality, though dependent upon nature's reality? And since drama especially engages the actions of human nature and since by his very existence the poet is a person, how may he through reason manage a making so that the made thing avoids being merely some segment of his personal history? That has been the poet's difficulty especially exacerbated in relation to the evolving Modernist doctrine of autonomy. We especially pointed to this difficulty as dramatized by James Joyce in his *Portrait of the Artist as a Young Man*, in respect to which that famous work might be considered an end rather than a beginning of "Modern" literature.

Here in brief then some remarks on T. S. Eliot and his difficulty with this dilemma to the poet, for it is with considerable agony of intellect and of spirit that Eliot finds himself constricted by Modernist ideologies. At last he pursues a resolution through the work of St. Thomas. Eliot, in his "Hamlet and His Problems" (1919), finds Shakespeare's play flawed, largely because in the play as in the sonnets (he says) there is "stuff that the writer could not drag to light, contemplate, or manipulate into art." It is something personal and as yet unresolved, so that it prevents Shakespeare's finding effective "objective correlatives" suited to the possible and probable actions of his agents without his becoming emotionally entangled through that gnawing personal complication.

It is well to observe here that presently Eliot himself will be reading St. Thomas, a part of his concern being a necessity to come to terms with the "personal" as it may affect his own work. This is the period of his life as maker in which he is overtly anxious about his "individual talent" in relation to tradition. He seems haunted by a fear of entanglement of his "personality" in his made thing, which could only flaw the good of the thing he would make.

What Eliot will come to recognize is that the poet's responsibility to proportion in the made thing, in relation to the possible or probable as inevitably derived from his own actual and speculative experiences of existential reality as person, requires an accommodation of the personal to the act of making, not a denial of, a reluctance to accept, the personal to making. A dilemma may emerge, in which in order to avoid the personal the poet may rather choose to pursue an "objective" proportion in the thing he is making through making as a matter of mechanics. Through "objective correlatives" – so Eliot argues – he would depersonalize emotion. No accident, then, that at this point of his journey Eliot – addressing directly the necessity of a "depersonalization" – describes the "action which takes place" which we have called intellectual making with the aid of "a suggestive analogy" from physics. The imaginative act of making is like "the action which takes place when a bit of finely filiated platinum is introduced into a chamber containing oxygen and sulfur dioxide." This is in description of his "impersonal theory of poetry," in which action the poet's mind is "catalyst." "The mind of the poet is the shred of platinum," prior to which it

has served as "a receptacle for seizing and storing up num-
berless feelings, phrases, images" as "particles which can
unite to form a new compound. . . ." Hardly metaphors promising an organic poetry such as that Coleridge argues for.

Remembering Coleridge (as Eliot by implication is doing
in these early critical essays which reflect his intellectual
flight from his Romantic fathers), we might remark as of use
to us an important speculative address to the concept of the
imagination by a Thomistic realist with whom Eliot will
become acquainted. Especially helpful in regard to the imagination as it must engage reality at a level deeper than
"impersonalization" in approaching the possible or probable.
Jacques Maritain in his Mellon Lectures, *Creative Intuition in
Art and Poetry* (1953) enlarges upon the Thomistic perspective. In Chapter Four of the published version, "Creative
Intuition and Poetic Knowledge," he is specifically concerned
to address Eliot's pre-*Waste Land* confidence that the poet can
control his own emotion in the making of poetry by a "scientific" intentionality. The argument of these Mellon Lectures
gains a larger metaphysical support in relation to that earlier
of his works generally known under the title *The Degrees of
Knowledge*. (That work's full title suggests its importance to
our pursuit of beauty: *Distinguish to Unite; or, The Degrees of
Knowledge*, tr. by Gerald B. Phelan.) Maritain, in his "Preface"
to the original edition (1932), remarks it an exposition of
"Thomistic realism," in which he recognizes that the "'philosophy of being' is at once, and *par excellence*, 'philosophy of
mind.'"

Concerning the teleological operations whereby intellect
must "distinguish to unite" in pursuit of a simple visionary
knowing (Maritain's book is a formidable almost 500-page
attempt), we might reflect that the exercise of detachment
through intentionality – whether as philosopher or poet –
requires objective (*distinguishing*) reasoning toward *correlative*
participation in creation itself. The intent for the philosopher
is to gain an understanding to be shared. For the poet it is
rather an enactment of the possible or probable in relation to

which emotions may be shared by poet and his listener. That is a depth of understanding in the term to which Eliot has at last arrived at the time Maritain publishes his *Degrees of Knowledge*. Eliot's Norton Lectures, *The Use of Poetry and the Use of Criticism*, are delivered in 1932–33 just as Maritain's book appears, and in his own lectures Eliot pays tribute to Maritain, some of whose work he has himself translated and published in his *Criterion*. Eliot's earlier confidence was in a "scientific" objectivity (whose analogy he finds in chemistry), which could serve to "depersonalize" his making and protect the maker from the risks of the emotions he intentionally stirs: that confidence is long since faded. (He will speak with self-deprecation after "Ash-Wednesday" of such popular terms in literary criticism as his "objective correlative" and the "dissociation of sensibilities," terms earlier engaged at the surface level and not in their metaphysical depths.) In his Norton Lectures as well there occurs a reconciliation of Eliot to his Romantic fathers – to Wordsworth and Coleridge, but he now especially values Keats.

It is in his recovered appreciation of Keats that we may perhaps most succinctly suggest a recovery to Eliot of his own sensibilities, an adumbration of that journey revealing Eliot's discoveries to be largely out of his own increasing "Thomistic realism." As for that earlier anticipation of and attempted exercise of a detached impersonality through an intentional science of the "objective correlative," Eliot can now see that something of the desired immediacy of the made thing, through the poet's participation by surrender to the good of the thing made, has been lost. (As a footnote to that recognition, consider the changing role of "masks" for Eliot as maker occurring between his "Love Song of J. Alfred Prufrock" and "Ash-Wednesday.) To put the point in Keatsian terms, the poet's participation of surrender to his making through "negative capability" is strained when a reasoned fear of personal risk in the making obtains. For the "aesthetic" concern for "depersonalization" is more complex than it seemed to Eliot in 1920. He is in reaction to a sentimentality destructive of the good of things made through an excessive surrender. That is the "Romanticism" he fears. Seeing a failure of reason to distinguish and then unite, Eliot chooses that alternate extreme in reaction to "Romantic" excesses of emotion. He cultivates a witty skepticism of detachment. But if Romantic excesses of commitment (often in reaction to Rationalism's obverse excess) damages made things in a disregard of "due proportion" (Thomas's phrase), ironic detachment may prove to hide an indifference under an aesthetic mask, rather than signifying a reasoned objectivity about the good of the thing being made. This is a point addressed in *Little Gidding*, III, occasioning the emergence of Dame Julian of Norwich within the lines by the way.

Not *due proportion* by *intentional exorcism of person* from the maker – a removal through depersonalization – then, seems afoot. For by a strict empirical science of knowing – a severe distinguishing whose effect is a separation rather than an accommodating unity with the making – the poet may be self-lured into form *imposed,* yielding a dead proportionality. It is a difference between what Coleridge (and the later Eliot) would distinguish as a mechanistic as opposed to an "organic" unity in the made thing. We have seen Joyce's Stephen "Romantically" pursuing just this course as a "young" artist with an intention to determine the thing he makes through intense will. We may well recall that both Eliot and Ezra Pound reacted to the 19th century's decaying of prosody by their attempt at a more organic response to the science proper to sound – recovered in the human voice and its patterns of speech. Pound, in reflective retrospect, recalls that his and Eliot's first "heave" in rescuing poetry was the overthrow of the iambic pentameter line which had become a domineering metronome. Both Pound and Eliot are learning the virtues of proportionality as that concept is a concern to St. Thomas in respect to art, though Pound will not pursue that concern in Thomas as Eliot does. (See Eliot's Clarke Lectures at Trinity College, Cambridge, in 1926, published after his death as *The Varieties of Metaphysical Poetry.* And in his Charles Eliot

Norton Lectures of Harvard, published as *The Use of Poetry and the Use of Criticism,* 1933, he pays special tribute to Maritain's *Art and Scholasticism.*) Eliot will dramatize the Modernist intellect as disoriented, and he would do so increasingly through a Keatsian "negative capability," requiring a present voice in his poem which earlier he had been fearful would be too much his own, whereby the poem may become constricted by the personal actual. This is the change in his understanding affecting the shift in his use of the "mask." Who speaks the lines? With "Ash-Wednesday" the answer becomes "Eliot," but it is a voice vatic – Eliot as *homo viator.*

That is the concern afoot, with some confusions to our response, in his "Hollow Men" and in *The Waste Land.* His making requires a proportionate ordering of the possible and probable disorder of the Modernist intellect in its responses to the world impinging upon Eliot as himself a Modernist, in relation to which he knows himself increasingly to be fundamentally dislocated as intellect and as person. And so in his early criticism we find his essays as "byproducts" of the poet's workshop, in which a common thematic concern is with the dangers of the personal to the good of the thing the poet would make. The dilemma is real to the poet and especially to the poet besieged by Modernism. Thus Joyce wonders whether he has become a poet of the fancy rather than of the imagination in his own attempts. Pound at the end of his *Cantos* wonders whether that work "coheres" (i.e., reveals a due proportion proper to his making). So too does Eliot begin to wonder, but he does so in the middle of his way, turning then to Thomas, especially as adumbrated by Maritain in *Art and Scholasticism.*

What Eliot comes to accept is that the person of the poet as maker must achieve an accommodation *beyond* the merely "impersonal." Thus the possible or probable, speaking an action of his own "personal" nature as disoriented, must not reject but accommodate that personal grounding of the possible or probable. It is, indeed, in this accommodation that dramatically the "negative capability" of the poet allows his entering into the thing he makes and thereby distorting due proportion. He need not deny the openness of love of himself as *person* making the thing in imitation of human nature's common actions. In doing so, his judgment of the proper "objective correlatives" suited to his making is governed by his "negative capability," the Keatsian lesson Eliot discovers. The argument must be put cryptically here, but I have pursued it at length in my *Making: The Proper Habit of Our Being*. And in respect to Eliot specifically as maker, and his pursuit of a recovery of the personal (evident in his "Ash-Wednesday" and especially in his *Four Quartets*) I engage this theme in *T. S. Eliot and the Still Point of Consciousness: An Excursion into the Four Quartets*.

B) Concerning Jacques Maritain's *Art and Scholasticism*, this small work was first published in English at Dichling, the seat of Eric Gill's and Hilery Pepler's Catholic "Community," in 1923. It had first appeared in French in 1920. Translated by Father John O'Connor, it was first issued under the title *The Philosophy of Art*. The year before – in the year of Eliot's *Waste Land* – Fr. O'Connor had received G. K. Chesterton into the Church, and the year before that David Jones. (Father O'Connor is the model for Chesterton's Father Brown mysteries.) In 1927 Gill reissued the work from St. Dominic's Press, adding to it Maritain's "The Frontiers of Poetry." Maritain's revised and final version came in 1935, *Frontieres de la poesie et autres essais*, which is the text used by Joseph W. Evans for his translation, published by Notre Dame Press as *Art and Scholasticism and the Frontiers of Poetry*, 1962.

The work was fundamentally important to Eric Gill and those gathered about him, especially David Jones, whose important poems *In Parenthesis* (1937), with an introduction by Eliot, and *Anathemata* (1952), published at Eliot's insistence, show Maritain's influence. In 1926, Eric Gill published a small book arguing the central Thomistic thesis, *Id Quod Visum Placet: A Practical Test of the Beautiful*. It is an "essay," he says in his "apology" to the reader, presented in the "consecrated" form of the Thomist articles of the *Summa Theologiae*. Maritain's arguments, then, became a continuing influence on English and American letters, including effects on Chesterton's Distributists, between whom and the Vanderbilt Agrarians there is a community of concern affected by this attention to the nature of the Beautiful in relation to the viability of community itself. Not only the Chestertonian Distributists were influenced. (St. Dominic's Press had reissued Belloc's *Servile State* in the 1920s, the work from which Distributist arguments proceeded.) In recent letters the relation of art to Thomistic scholasticism proved important to T. S. Eliot, Allen Tate, Caroline Gordon, Flannery O'Connor, Walker Percy, and many others.

C) In the *Summa Theologiae*, Pt I–II, Q 26, A 1, Reply Objection 3, Thomas responds to an insufficient use of Dionysius in Objection 3. Natural love, he says, "is not only in the powers of the vegetal soul, but in all the soul's powers, and also in all the parts of the body, and universally in all things: because, as Dionysius says (*Div. Nom.* iv), *Beauty and goodness are beloved by all things*; since each single thing has a connaturalness with that which is naturally suitable to it." The ground to that connaturality is being itself, each single thing created in that context to the singularity of existing things. And in defense of St. Augustine's declaration that "Assuredly, the good alone is beloved" and is therefore the cause of love, Thomas says (Q. 27, Reply Objection 3):

> The beautiful is the same as the good, and they differ in aspect only [i.e., differ by a difference of intellectual perspective upon the good]. For since good is what all seek, the notion of good is that which calms desire; while the notion of the beautiful is that which calms the desire, by being seen or known. Consequently those senses chiefly regard the beautiful, which are the most cognitive, viz., sight and hearing, as ministering to reason; for we speak of beautiful sights and beautiful sounds. But in reference to other objects of the other senses, we do not use the

expression *beautiful*, for we do not speak of beautiful tastes, and beautiful odors. Thus it is evident that beauty adds to goodness in relation to the cognitive faculty: so that *good* means that which simply pleases the appetite; while the beautiful is something pleasant to apprehend.

D) See also: *Summa Theologiae* I–II, Q 57, Art 3: "Art is nothing else but *the right reason about certain works to be made.*" And I–II, Q 57, Art 4: "art is the *right reason of things to be made;* whereas prudence is the *right reason of things to be done.*"

E) Gilson, "Love and the Passions," *The Christian Philosophy of St. Thomas Aquinas* (1956), regarding St. Thomas's remark that beauty is that which when seen pleases:

> As a definition, it is true, but it contributes to [a] misconception we should try to avoid. Beautiful colors and beautiful forms are those which are pleasing to sight. But it is not enough that the sight of them please for them to be beautiful. There is no aesthetic joy whose cause is not in the beauty of the object. We know now in what this beauty consists. The joy it gives is a joy *sui generis*, the distinctive quality of which we all know from experience. This is the radiance with which certain perfect acts of knowing are surrounded, and which confers on certain acts of sensible knowledge the very character of contemplation. Then too is born the love of beauty, the complacency of a knowing faculty in an object in which the act which apprehends it finds, along with its ultimate contentment, its perfect repose (275).

Also important to this general argument: Gilson's *Forms and Substances in the Arts*, 1964, and Maritain's *Creative Intuition in Art and Poetry*, 1953